Journey to Joy

Insights and Actions for a Happier Life

By Susan Goryeb Simms, LCSW

The author of this book does not dispense medical advice or prescribe the use of any technique as a form of treatment for physical, emotional, or medical problems without the advice of a physician, either directly or indirectly. The intent of the author is only to offer information of a general nature to help you in your quest for emotional and spiritual well-being. In the event you use any of the information in this book for yourself, which is your constitutional right, the author, and the publisher assumes no responsibility for your actions.

The clients presented in this book are a composite of the many clients the author has treated and any identifying information is coincidental.

ISBN: 1544796382

ISBN-13: 978-1544796383

Cover design by Kevin and Jessica Simms.
Artwork by Kevin Simms.

Dedication

I dedicate this book to my husband Kevin, and my children, Jess and Nick. They are my greatest source of love and joy, and they inspire me each and every day with their wisdom, passion, and compassion.

Table of Contents

Acknowledgements

I am incredibly grateful to all of the people who helped to make this book a reality. I have been a "student" my whole life, always reading and trying to understand the mysteries of life. I am grateful for all of the great minds that have put pen to paper to allow all of us in on the secrets of a happier, more joyful life. I am also grateful for the current research that is being done on happiness, which provides scientific proof to help even the biggest skeptics give it a try.

To my husband, Kevin, thank you for being my greatest support. I am so lucky to share this journey with you. Your tireless editing, designing, and formatting, not to mention your beautiful artwork, have allowed me to publish a book that I am proud of. Without your technical knowledge and talent, this book would not exist. Kevin, you, and our children, Jessica and Nicholas, are my greatest source of joy. Jess and Nick, you inspire me with your passions, not only in the arts that you pursue but also in your desire to make the world a better place; your support and love are woven throughout the pages of this book. Kevin and Jessica, thank you for your beautiful cover design and artwork and for bringing my vision to life.

To Janice Fuchs, my mentor and coach, you have consistently encouraged me to publish my work and helped me to believe that I had something important to say. I am incredibly grateful for your friendship and support as well as your gentle, and not so gentle, nudges to write and publish.

To all of my friends and family who offer support and joy to me. You are all such an important part of my life, and whether I speak to you daily, monthly or yearly, you are a source of inspiration, support, love, and joy. My life is so much richer because of each of you.

Finally, to all of my clients, I thank you for sharing your stories with me and trusting me to help you along your journey. Each of you inspires me with your strength, courage, and resilience. Your ability to "journey to joy" has been an honor and joy for me as well.

Preface

"Life is a journey, not a destination."

— *Ralph Waldo Emerson*

If life is a journey, we may as well make it a joyful one. Google defines joy as a feeling of great pleasure and happiness. What a way to live your life—with a feeling of great pleasure and happiness! Isn't that what everyone wants? However, joy seems to be elusive for many. Living a joyless life is far too common. In a society where stress is a way of life, how do we make room for joy? How can we bring more joy to our lives while we minimize our levels of stress?

As a psychotherapist for more than twenty-five years, I have heard these questions asked in many different ways, and I have made it my life's work to help people create more joy in their lives. That, after all, is the goal of therapy; to help people lead happier, more joyful lives.

When I graduated from Columbia University School of Social Work in 1990, I felt that my training would assist me in becoming an effective therapist. But as a therapist, like in many jobs, you continue to learn on the job every day. And I discovered that my education on the workings of joy had only just begun.

From the time I was very young, I had a sense of empathy and compassion and a passion for helping others. People seemed to feel naturally comfortable talking to me about their problems. I gladly listened and offered support and validation.

I remember watching a TV show called, "The Runaways" as a young teen. The show was about social workers that rescued runaway teens and helped them with their families. I remember thinking, "I want to do that. I want to be a social worker and help people too."

My dad, a very practical person, suggested that I consider another profession because I needed to support myself and social work didn't pay well. Ironically, although my dad was an accountant, he too was a naturally compassionate listener and spent a lot of time counseling his clients on many issues, not just their finances.

I graduated with a degree in Communications and began my career in the advertising, marketing, and publishing industries. After working in the "business world" for a couple of years, I felt a deep sense of emptiness in my work. It was interesting and creative work at times, but it lacked the meaning that I was seeking. So, I returned to school and got my master's degree in social work. That was my calling. That is where my heart was.

I always tried to be the best at whatever I did. So, as an intellectual person, I went where I always went...to the bookstore. I read book after book on everything important to me. I was always looking for answers not only for myself but my clients as well.

When my children were young, I remember reading many parenting books. The best books seemed to have the message that whatever you focus on you get more of. It seemed so obvious to me; focus on positive behavior and ignore negative behavior. I never connected with books about harsh discipline and punishment, so this philosophy felt right to me. At the same time, I was reading books about success. Wanting to build my practice and develop myself professionally. The message in these books seemed to be the same. Book after book on every subject appeared to have some version of this concept. I had stumbled upon the Law of Attraction. I began to read more and more about this magical law, and as I did, I noticed that things in my life started to change. I also started doing research on "Positive Psychology" and the science of happiness. It was fascinating. I'd discovered that a lot of things that I had been doing in my life that made me feel better, had scientific backing. I read as much as I could and practiced it as often as possible.

I was fortunate enough to have been trained in a variety of forms of psychotherapy. My eclectic approach allowed me to find what worked best with each client. In working with my clients, I noticed that some didn't respond well to traditional psychotherapy methods alone. As I read and learned more, then applied what I learned to my life, the way I helped my clients began to change as well. By combining everything I learned with strength-based supportive therapy, I became some combination of a therapist, life coach, and spiritual advisor. Whatever it was, the results started to feel like nothing short of magic. My practice began to multiply. Many of my clients had been in therapy before, and either had bad experiences or just didn't make progress. I watched as they transformed before my eyes. They made progress quickly, and they loved sharing their joy with me.

In this book, I will share with you what I have learned. I will share personal stories as well as some from my clients that illustrate why and how applying the Law of Attraction and making other small changes can help you create a more joyful life. My goal is to reach more people and spread the joy. There are many books on managing stress and creating a better life. I have read hundreds of them, and many have similar information. And yet still, I get something different from every book I read. Each book motivates me in a different way. This book is just my perspective on this vast pool of information and my experiences over the years. I always say that even if the information isn't new, sometimes you can hear something in a new way that helps you to get it. I hope you have that experience with *Journey to Joy*. I have included "Joyful Action Steps" at the end of each chapter to help you every step of the way. Thank you for joining me on this journey.

Joyfully yours,

Susan

What is the Law of Attraction?

"You are actually pre-paving your future experiences constantly...You are continually projecting your expectations into your future experiences."

— *Esther Hicks*

The Law of Attraction has been taught by some of the greatest minds of all time for centuries. Every successful person practices it, and it is the answer to why people have the lives they do (whether they know it or not). Simply put, the Law of Attraction states that whatever you focus on you get more of. If you focus on problems, you get more problems. If you focus on success, you get more success. If you focus on lack, you will be sure to experience more lack. Using the Law of Attraction to your advantage is one of the foundations of creating a more joyful life. Time and time again, I have seen the Law of Attraction working both for and against people, and I have personally experienced it over and over. Consider that you are like a magnet, and you will draw to you whatever you direct the magnet towards.

As an example of how the law works, I'd like to share a story with you. A couple of years ago we installed a new patio in our backyard. We had a small fire pit and made a little area for it. I kept looking and thinking that I would like to have some curved benches around it. Every time I sat out back, I would look over and imagine the fire pit with benches around it. I just thought it would look nice. I started looking online and saw lots of benches, but they cost more than I wanted to spend. Plus the shipping was almost as much as the bench. But I still found myself looking. One weekend, my husband and I were driving home from a walk at the pond, and we spotted a sign for a moving sale. We decided to check it out. When we got there, the homeowner announced that all of the outdoor furniture had been sold. My husband and I looked around at the other items in the house and were about to leave. My husband asked, "So, you sold all of the outdoor furniture?" The woman responded that the person who was going to buy it just called to say she couldn't come, so if we wanted to check it out, we could go in the backyard. As we opened the gate, the first thing I noticed was four curved benches around a tree. I asked how much they were, and she said she would take $10 each. Sold! That is the Law of Attraction in action. I'll be honest; I wasn't even thinking about the benches when we got there. But I had thought about them and imagined them so vividly, that soon they were manifested.

When I tell stories like this, I often hear that "it is just a coincidence." Maybe that's true, but I have experienced these "coincidences" over and over. So, why is it that some people are so good at having coincidences like this happen? And why is it that those who understand the Law of Attraction are so inclined to have these coincidences? I like to share stories like this with my clients and watch as their interest is piqued. They always want to try it out for themselves. Then the stories come in. I love seeing how powerful people can be and watching them move into that power. There is so much to read about the Law of Attraction, and I encourage you to read up on the subject. I have included some of my favorites at the end of the book. Like so much of what I've learned in the past twenty years, many of the lessons and the techniques that I discuss have roots in the Law of Attraction.

Intention

"Excellence is never an accident. It is always the result of high intention, sincere effort, and intelligent execution; it represents the wise choice of many alternatives - choice, not chance, determines your destiny."

— *Aristotle*

Intention is a powerful concept. Every action we take, from getting out of bed in the morning to brushing our teeth to getting a job starts with an intention. Intention is the first step to getting you from where you are to where you want to be. So if you want to make a change, it helps to set the intention of that change. Intention is, in essence, a commitment. So let us start by setting the intention to create a more joyful life.

Think about the areas of your life that are important to you and decide what you'd like to see more of in each area. As you think of each area (family, friends, career, home, spirituality, health, etc.) take a moment to decide how you would like these aspects of your life to look. Imagine in your mind and get a clear image of how you could make each of these areas more joyful. What will you be doing differently with your family when you are more joyful? How will you act at work when you are more joyful? Without an intention, it's hard to know where you are headed. I like to write it out and sign it. Your intention becomes like a contract for what you plan to do—live a more joyful life. The next chapter contains an exercise to help you visualize this more clearly.

Intention is, in many ways, a request you send to the universe. I have found, time and time again, that the simple act of setting an intention puts in motion a chain of events leading to the materialization of that intention. Whatever you choose to do will create change, positive or negative, depending on the intention.

As an employee assistance counselor, I trained in solution-focused therapy. I learned that change often occurs *before* the first session, after calling for an appointment. The thinking behind this is that once someone makes the decision to seek help, they begin the *process* of creating change. The minute they set the intention, change begins.

I use this power in so many ways in my work and my life. Studies by the Japanese scientist, Masaru Emoto, show how intention physically changes the structure of water[1]. He placed words on beakers of water and then froze the water and examined it under a microscope. Each word had its own, unique crystalline structure. Positive words like "love" and "peace" had beautiful snowflake-like patterns. However negative words like "hate" or "Hitler" looked murky and lacked a definite design. Emoto just placed the words on the beakers, which set the intention of each word on the water within. I find his work to be fascinating, and I share it with my clients often. It's important to know that the intention of different words impacts the object of that intention.

In another experiment, Emoto put rice in three different beakers and covered the rice with water. The first beaker had the words, "I love you," the second beaker had the words, "You're an idiot," and the third beaker said, "Ignore." For thirty days as he passed the beakers of water he did as it said. Saying, "I love you" to the first, "You're an idiot" to the second and ignoring the third. At the end of the thirty days, the first beaker began to ferment, giving off a sweet

---

[1] *Watch Masaru Emoto's experiment at* https://www.youtube.com/watch?v=tAvzsjcBtx8

aroma. The second beaker turned black, and the rice in the third beaker began to rot. Of course, I had to try this out myself, and I had similar results. Think about that when you are using words to speak to yourself or others. Words, or at least the intention of those words, have an impact on the recipient.

In light of water's ability to be altered with intention, I like to recommend that while showering you set the intention that, as the water washes over you, it is taking away all of your worries as well. Anything that doesn't serve you or that causes you pain can wash down the drain along with the water and the soap. Such visualization can be very powerful. But don't stop there! After all of your negative emotions have been released, you can then imagine that the water is healing any pain—physical or emotional—that you may be experiencing. Imagine the water protecting you from any negativity you may encounter that day, like a shield or a force field. Visualize and create this intention each and every day, and see if you don't feel a little lighter.

I love the smell of rosewater, and I keep a small spray bottle of it in my office. When I fill the bottle, I set the intention of healing, peace, and joy. Before I begin seeing clients each day I spray the office and again set the intention for my office to be infused with these properties to create an environment where healing can take place. I know that I feel the difference, and I believe my clients feel it as well. Many years ago I was working with a young woman, and one day she brought a friend with her. When she walked into the room, she said to her friend, "Can't you feel the healing when you walk in the door?" I also use a spray in my home to promote a peaceful environment. You can do this with any scent you love. All it takes is a spray bottle, some water, a little essential oil and an intention. You can make several different room sprays with different intentions. Use them in the air, or you can mist them on yourself, to wash away negativity or surround yourself with relaxation or joy.

When I am working with couples, I make sure that they set the intention to have a better relationship at the start of therapy. Often there is an unspoken intention to prove that the other person is at fault. They want a mediator who will convince their partner how right they are. If we don't set the intention for connection early on, we can end up with a session of each of them blaming the other. That is far less productive than working towards a happier relationship.

This power of intention can be used in so many ways. Anytime you want to create positive change, set the intention, and you will be automatically moving in the direction you want. For now, let's focus on creating a more joyful life. The minute you purchased this book, you set this intention in motion. Throughout the following chapters, you will have the opportunity to think about various aspects of your life. I encourage you to keep an open mind and know that the more joyful life you wish for is already on its way.

Joyful Action Steps: Intention

Close your eyes and take a deep breath in through your nose and out through your mouth. Repeat this several times until you feel calm and relaxed. Try to relax your body and still your mind to allow for clearer intentions.

Now answer the following questions to the best of your ability based on where you are right now.

1. Why do I want to feel more joyful?

    _____

    _____

2. Who (other than me) will benefit from my feeling more joyful?

    _____

    _____

3. I am setting the intention to feel greater joy in my life because of the above reasons and because it will benefit others as well as me. When my life is more joyful it will look a little like this: (visualization exercise in next section)

4. Wash away negativity and surround yourself with healing during your shower by setting the intention.

5. Create a "calm spray" or a "joy spray" and use it often in your home or on yourself.

Visualization

"Imagination is everything. It is the preview of life's coming attractions."

— *Albert Einstein*

After you set your intention, it's time to get busy visualizing this intention in action. Imagination is another powerful tool. Imagine what you want in your life. Visualize everything with as much detail as you can. Whatever you can see, you can create. The late Napoleon Hill said: "Whatever your mind can conceive and believe the mind can achieve regardless of how many times you may have failed in the past." I ask my clients to think about their perfect life. What does it look like? Describe it in great detail. No limits…do not hold back!

If I had a magic wand, and I told you tomorrow you would wake up in your perfect life, what would it look like? How would you be different? With whom would you spend time? What would you be doing? How would you feel? Do this with as much detail as you possibly can. You would be amazed at how often this becomes a reality. I do this periodically, and I am often shocked when I look back and see how much I've created that was in my description. My clients have done this with incredible success as well.

One client that stands out is an attractive woman in her early thirties who had recently divorced. She was devastated by this loss of the love of her life. She proclaimed herself a very positive person. She said she tried to be upbeat, and from all appearances, she was. She was funny, and she smiled a lot. But she was not feeling optimistic about her life. Her job, her living situation and the dating world were all miserable to her. When she first came in, she said, "I really don't know how you can help me. You can't change my circumstances, but I figured I have nothing to lose." So, week after week, she let me know how bad her life was, and any attempts I made to offer hope were shot down with, "Yeah that sounds good, but that's not the way it works for me." Or she would smile and say, "Yeah, but there are no good guys out there." Then she would show me profiles of men on her dating site and explain all the things wrong with them. Her insistence that things couldn't get better and things didn't work out for her kept her from seeing all of the possibilities available to her.

When she first came in, I asked her to write a detailed description of the life she wanted in the present tense as I described earlier. When she brought it in the following week, I was impressed with her writing. She used so much detail I had to question whether any of it had actually happened. I asked her how she felt when she read it, and she replied, "It makes me want to cry... It's so far from what my life looks like that it's depressing." I explained to her that I really could see her life looking like that. I didn't see why it couldn't happen for her. Why couldn't she be happy and have the life that she dreamed of? She said that none of the guys she dated were right for her. And I assured her that that's always the way it is. It's always wrong until it's right, it doesn't work until it does. Ask anyone who met their dream mate, and they will always say that all the people they dated before were wrong—until they met the *right* person. I told her that even if she didn't have hope for that, I did! I believed that it could happen for her too…maybe even today or tomorrow she would meet "Mr. Right." At that moment, I saw a glimmer of hope in her eyes. It was the first time she didn't try to fight me on it.

The next time I saw her, I opened the door to my waiting room, and I knew something had changed. The smile on her face seemed more genuine than usual. She looked truly happy! I asked her how she was and she replied, "Really great actually!" She proceeded to tell me about the man she met, and how she felt completely connected to him. He felt the same way about her. He just so happened to have all the qualities she put in her "Perfect Life Story." They had already seen each other several times, and he was a big believer in the "Law of Attraction." We met three more times for a total of eight sessions. She was feeling better about every aspect of her life by then and was extremely grateful for whatever "magic" happened in my office.

Several months later I received a message from her telling me that she had gotten engaged, and was planning her wedding and honeymoon. She got a new job that she enjoyed, and it paid much better, and she was in the process of moving into a new apartment. "Basically everything I wrote in that 'perfect life' description had come completely true…like magic." She said she continues to practice using the Law of Attraction and the power of visualization to create her wonderful life.

Over the years, I've shared her story with other clients, and they too become motivated to write their "perfect life" story. I love watching the look on their faces when they hear about how it can work and seeing them imagining their own amazing lives and finding joy as they materialize. Sometimes my clients get discouraged along the way until I remind them of the changes they've created, and then they get right back on track.

Visualization is such a powerful tool. We use it all the time whether we know it or not. Unfortunately, we often inadvertently visualize the opposite of what we want. Many people get stuck in 'worst case scenarios' and go there automatically, which can lead to feelings of fear and anxiety or even hopelessness.

Our bodies are affected by the images in our heads more than you may realize. Try this exercise: Close your eyes and imagine a big yellow lemon. Imagine cutting the lemon in half. It's very juicy! Now imagine squeezing the juice onto your tongue. If you are like many people, your mouth may start to water, or your face might scrunch up as though you just ate the lemon. And yet these are only words on a page that create an image in your mind.

So why would we use this incredible power to imagine things that cause us so much pain and sadness when we could use this power to create so much good?

Successful athletes know the power of visualization and often use it to create success. They visualize themselves winning. Coaches draw pictures of plays on a blackboard so players can imagine them taking place. As a teenager, I remember using this technique without even realizing it. I had been taking tennis lessons and one day I bought a tennis magazine. I remember reading the magazine at night and learning about different techniques for a better backhand. I didn't have a racquet in my room, but as I read about an interesting technique, I naturally imagined it in my mind. The next time I played, my backhand was much better. I had practiced *in my mind.*

So make a pact with yourself to imagine the best. You can't create a better life for yourself if you can't imagine it. Instead of imagining the worst-case scenario, imagine the *best*-case scenario. Start creating a more joyful life—starting with your mind.

Joyful Action Steps: Visualization

Close your eyes and take a deep breath. As you exhale, imagine that all of the stress and strain of your life is leaving. As you inhale, you are breathing in the calm and joyful feelings that you desire. Now let's return to the imagery of the magic wand. Imagine that you have a fairy godmother or a Genie in a bottle that is granting you the life of your dreams. The Genie asks you to imagine the life you desire. You don't need to limit it to three things. Imagine every aspect of your life is exactly the way you want: your job, your health, your family, your home, etc. You have the life you truly desire. You experience joy every day. You are filled with the feeling of peace and joy. What does that look like? What does it *feel* like? What are you doing every day? Where are you working, and who do you spend time with? Imagine this as clearly and vividly as you can.

Now that you have fully imagined your joyful life write it out in the present tense with as much detail as possible…the more descriptive the better. Use as much detail and feeling as you can. No one is grading you. No one even needs to see it. It is for you. You can write it in a journal or write in this book. At the very end of the story, finish with the words, "Or something better," just in case there is something better than you can imagine waiting for you. Don't lose what you wrote because you will want to refer to it in the future to see how you created this incredible life.

My Perfect Life Story

_____

_____

_____

_____

_____

_____

_____

_____

_____

_____

_____

_____

_____

_____

_____

_____

_____

_____

_____

_____

Gratitude

"Gratitude unlocks the fullness of life. It turns what we have into enough, and more. It turns denial into acceptance, chaos to order, confusion to clarity. It can turn a meal into a feast, a house into a home, a stranger into a friend."

— *Melody Beattie*

There is a reason why everywhere you turn you hear about the power of gratitude. I believe so strongly in the importance of gratitude in a joyful life because I feel that there is no joy without gratitude. You cannot experience joy with an absence of gratitude. It *cannot* be done!

I have used many different things to keep track of my gratitude or to remind myself to be grateful. After the movie *The Secret* came out, I carried a rock in my pocket, and every time I reached into my pocket, I thought about something for which I was grateful. I've kept gratitude journals, and I've written lists of things I was grateful for in my phone. One time I was reading a book about Feng Shui, the Chinese practice of placing things in particular areas to affect the energy in the home. It suggested placing a gratitude bowl in the center of the house, then writing down what you are grateful for and placing it in the bowl. My family and I would write what we were thankful for on slips of paper and watch as the bowl filled with gratitude.

I don't care how you decide to do it but just do it. Take time to appreciate the good in your life. I promise you it will make you a happier person, and you will be nicer to be around as well. Several years ago, I was going through an extremely painful and difficult time. I felt very alone. One day, I sat down and made a list of everyone that expressed concern or caring during that time. It didn't matter if the people listed were able to help or even if they said the wrong thing. I just focused on the fact that they cared. I listed family members, neighbors, the pharmacist, acquaintances, anyone and everyone that cared. I also wrote down *how* they showed that they cared. Sometimes they showed it in a big way, and sometimes it was in a small way, but everything counted. The list was so much longer than I would have thought. I looked at that list, and I didn't feel alone anymore. I felt incredibly supported. In the past, I may have focused on who didn't call to check in, or that 'nobody' cared. I wouldn't have noticed how much good was present. I would have felt more resentful, more alone and angrier. But instead, I focused on my gratitude for what I had. I definitely felt much better, and not surprisingly, things started to get better.

Many years ago, I had a client who was having problems with his wife. He came in with his electronic planner (it was a *long* time ago), and he read to me all the things his wife did that bothered him. He literally documented everything she did that got on his nerves. He came in and rattled them off. They were really small things like, "She bought the wrong kind of cookies." Little things can get on your nerves; it's very true. But focusing on them and documenting them will never lead to a better relationship. I discussed this with him and suggested that he look for all the good things she did for him, and document that instead. I told him to delete the negative list, which was a constant reminder to him of all the things he didn't like. He reluctantly agreed. He began to appreciate his wife more. Within a short time, his relationship had improved greatly.

When you are struggling with someone you love, someone who is important to you (a spouse, a child, a parent), try making a list of all of his or her good qualities as a reminder to you. Relationships can be hard. Living with people can be hard. We can all get on each other's nerves from time to time. Here is a great exercise to help remind you of all of the good inside of these important people. List things they've done that have brightened your day or your life. List how you felt at various times in your life with them. Maybe it's the day you were married or the day you held your child for the first time. When you are struggling with their personality flaws, pull out the list to remind yourself of how much you love them. This technique works great for parents going through the teenage years with their kids.

Gratitude will transform your life! I have gotten into such a habit of gratitude that I find myself thinking or saying the words "thank you" too many times a day to count. I am grateful for the beauty of nature over and over. I get excited about little things like the sparkles of light on the water and how the sun shines. I'm grateful when things went well when I wasn't sure they would. I'm appreciative of all of the happy moments with my family. Try being sad when you're focused on all of the gifts in your every day. If you can't find something to be grateful for, you aren't looking very hard.

I often think about people who survive horrible circumstances. We've all seen them and heard their stories. We hear about people going through unspeakable tragedy and coming out of it feeling grateful. Several years ago, during Hurricane Sandy, so many people lost everything they owned. I would watch the news stories and see the devastation, but what I found myself most drawn to was the appreciation that these people had despite all of their loss. Time and time again, you would see people hugging one another and saying they were grateful to be alive or that some small item was spared. In every disaster and tragedy, take the time to notice the people that rise above, and the outpouring of support that they are so thankful for. Then think again if you can't find something to be grateful for in your life. If I'm having one of those days when I am not able to feel grateful, I always remind myself of that. It doesn't take long to move into a grateful state.

There has been a lot of research on the benefit of gratitude and its effect on happiness. There is scientific proof of its power. Of all the things I teach my clients, I am convinced that focusing on being more grateful is the most important thing you can do to experience greater joy. I know it has been true for me. Gratitude is tied in with compassion, love, mindful wonder, forgiveness, positive focus and connection. It makes all of these things easier.

If you are looking to develop a gratitude habit, consider this: Supposedly, it takes 21 days for a new habit to take hold. Every day for 21 days, scan your world for three things you are grateful for. Be specific and use as much detail as possible (remember the power of visualization). Doing so will create a mindset in which you are looking for good. It's important to look for *new* things every day because you want to be *searching* for things to be thankful for. So yes, while you may be thankful for your health and your family every day, that isn't going to create a different mindset of *looking* for things to be grateful for.

You can use the rock method, the journal method, the bowl method or even your phone. Any method of acknowledging your gratitude will work. I hope you develop this habit because it feels much better than looking for all the things that are *wrong* with the world and your life. I've done both, and looking for the good feels a whole lot better.

Once you make the decision to be more grateful, you are opening your mind and your heart and transforming your life. It is as if you are seeing the world in color for the first time. Everything looks brighter and more beautiful. If you only make one change after reading this book, let this be it. Gratitude is the greatest gift you can give yourself and others. Once you start, you won't want to stop. Gratitude will propel you to joy faster than anything else you do.

Joyful Action Steps: Gratitude

Gratitude work: Choose one or more of the following methods of experiencing gratitude and begin today.

1. **Gratitude Journal** – Write three (or more) things every day that you noticed during the past day that you appreciate or are grateful for. Do not choose the same three things every day. Be sure to look for things to appreciate throughout the day.

2. **Gratitude Stone** – Go for a walk and look for a nice stone that you can use as a "gratitude stone" or buy a pretty crystal or stone for the same purpose. Carry the stone with you each day. When you reach into your pocket, remember to feel gratitude for something that you experienced that day. Alternatively, you can leave a stone on your desk at work, in your kitchen, or in your bedroom as a reminder to think about what you have to be grateful for.

3. **Beautiful People Lists** – Create a separate page for each significant person in your life. On each page list all of the wonderful things about that person. Make one for your significant other, each child, friend, parent, etc.—whoever you are in contact with. Doing so reminds you of all the good you have around you. Alternatively, you can make a list of all the people in your life that you are grateful for. List everyone and

why you are grateful for them. Include teachers from your past, your children's teachers, your neighbors, friends from the past that had an impact on your life (whether or not they are still in your life), etc.

4. **Thank You Letters** – Similar to the previous list, write personal letters or notes to people who have helped you at any time in your life. You can choose to send them or deliver them, which would be equally powerful for them, or you can choose to write them just for you if you do not wish to have that contact, or if they are no longer alive.

5. **Gratitude Jar/Bowl** – Keep a jar or bowl in the center of your home for the purpose of putting gratitude inside. Leave a little notepad and pen to write something down as it occurs to you and place it in the bowl or jar. Watch as the bowl/jar fills up with your gratitude.

Positive Focus

"In order to carry a positive action, we must develop here a positive vision."

— *Dalai Lama*

Tied in with gratitude is "positive focus." By this, I mean surrounding yourself with positivity. Read books about the Law of Attraction and happiness. Watch inspirational YouTube videos. Drown your newsfeed on Facebook with positive pages that send you positive messages and images (my Facebook Page **Positive Therapy 4 U** is one of them). Spend time with the people that make you feel good. Make lunch dates with friends that leave you feeling happy.

I remember my daughter's first-grade teacher talking about "immersing the children in words." All over the classroom, she had words with pictures attached hanging from the ceiling, and many items were labeled so the children would associate each word with its item. "That's how children learn to read," she would say. Brilliant!

Do that with positivity. Immerse yourself in it. Put sticky notes around your house with positive sayings. I love the new trend with wooden signs that have positive messages on them. I have several of them in my home as well as a chalkboard border on which I write positive messages. During one difficult time, I had on the board, "Whatever Happens I'll Handle It." Right now it says, "Things are Always Working Out for Me." One day, the father of one of my daughter's friends came over to pick her up. He noticed all of the positive signs around and commented how nice that was. Then he laughed and said that his wife would have one big sign that said, "Deal with it!" I had to laugh.

The point is that if you surround yourself with these positive ideas, they can sink in and counteract some of the automatic negative thoughts we have.

Positive affirmations are part of this immersion in positivity. Positive affirmations are statements in the present tense about how you want things to be. They should be specific, and detailed, and elicit a positive feeling. If you want to be more at peace and happy, a good affirmation might be, "I am calm and peaceful, and I live my life joyously." If you are trying to help yourself fight feelings of unworthiness, a good affirmation might be, "I am worthy of love, and I deserve kindness, especially from me."

At one time, I had a client named "Amanda" who struggled with feeling unworthy. I wrote down the affirmation, "I am worthy" and when she looked at it, she exclaimed, "That's what my name means! Amanda means worthy!" I thought that was so interesting! I told her that whenever she wrote her name or said, "I am Amanda," she was essentially saying, "I am worthy!" I told her to think of that whenever she thought of or spoke her name. What a beautiful validation to remind her daily.

There are many books on affirmations, and you can find many positive affirmations and messages with a simple Google search. As you find affirmations that you are drawn to, or that address a particular need, write them in a journal. Read them when you wake up in the morning and before you go to bed at night. Surround yourself with good thoughts and notice your feelings improve.

Joyful Action Steps: Positive Focus

1. Buy inspirational signs and place them prominently in your home.

2. Find quotes or sayings that make you feel good, and put them on sticky notes in areas of your home where you will see them.

3. Follow pages on Facebook, Instagram, or Twitter that offer feel-good messages rather than joy-zapping messages. **Positive Therapy 4 U** is my Facebook page with the sole purpose of providing positive messages.

4. Make a list of positive affirmations that are helpful for YOU to counter some of your automatic negative thoughts. Keep them handy for when those negative thoughts creep up on you. Read them every morning when you wake up, and every night before you fall asleep.

5. Watch positive videos that make you laugh or smile.

6. When you choose to watch TV, choose uplifting or funny shows.

7. Spend time with the people who lift you up. Spend most of your time with these joy-giving people.

Avoid Negativity

"Just think of any negativity that comes at you as a raindrop falling into the ocean of your bliss."

— *Maharishi Mahesh Yogi*

Obviously, if you are immersing yourself in positivity, it naturally follows that you should limit or eliminate as much negativity as you can. There are three categories of negativity.

Toxic People – You know who they are…the people that are always complaining, putting you or others down, and always finding the bad in every situation or the world in general. These are the people who, after spending time with them, you walk away feeling drained or bad about yourself or the world. They may find subtle ways to insult you. You don't always realize what's happening, but you walk away feeling worse than you did before you spoke to them. It could be a family member, a friend, a co-worker, or an acquaintance. If you must spend time with toxic people, try to limit that time as much as possible. Be sure to practice some self-care before and after. You will need the TLC. If you have a Facebook "friend" whose posts you find upsetting or disturbing, hide or unfriend them. You don't need to get worked up about other people's drama. Doing so is incredibly empowering.

Toxic Information – Again, this could be the information in your newsfeed on Facebook. Be diligent about filling your feed with information that makes you feel good, and limit the information that makes you feel bad. Limit watching the news, and instead read only the important information that you need. Many news shows thrive on drama and negativity. There is plenty of good that happens every day, so why is the bad news what we deem newsworthy? You might end up being a little less informed, but you will be happier.

Avoid upsetting TV shows. Your entertainment shouldn't cause you grief and anguish. Many years ago, I was in the habit of watching the TV show "ER." I enjoyed watching all the characters and their relationships. But, as a medical show, there was a lot of drama and trauma. At the time, I was working at a hospital in the Employee Assistance Program. I heard about real life drama daily, and at times I had to debrief the staff after particularly traumatic situations. That was part of the draw for me, I felt like an insider on the show. I knew about this stuff. I knew about the struggles that the nurses and doctors went through. However, as an extremely sensitive person, I would become very upset by some of the story lines. I would find myself crying and worked up at times. A dear friend of mine that I worked with told me she stopped watching the show because she was also very affected by it. She said it wasn't good for her to get so worked up from ten to eleven o'clock at night. It took me a little longer, but ultimately I did the same thing. It was hard to let go of the show, especially since everyone I worked with was watching and talking about it, but I felt much better after I did.

You have control over the information you receive. Choose what feels best.

Toxic Mind – I am sure this is the most important category in avoiding negativity. Although I encourage people to avoid negativity in their lives as much as possible, I am also aware that we cannot live in a bubble, avoiding everyone and everything that is not a positive influence. We will inevitably be required to deal with sources of stress throughout our lives. That is why it is so important to be aware of the toxic mind. The **toxic mind** refers to our negative thoughts that fuel our bad feelings. Most of us believe that other people and circumstances cause us pain, anger, frustration, anxiety, etc. But, in reality, it is our thoughts about these people and circumstances that cause these difficult or painful feelings.

Our thoughts determine our feelings every time. How you feel is always a reflection of how you think. I am not trying to say that different situations aren't more likely to elicit certain thoughts, but I *am* saying that how we choose to speak to ourselves in any situation has a huge bearing on how we feel at that time.

We are in a constant conversation with ourselves. We speak to ourselves automatically without even realizing it. By becoming aware of our self-talk, we have the ability to tweak it so we can feel more joyful. In any situation, there are a variety of thoughts that we can think. If we are generally in a toxic mindset, our thoughts will go to a negative place.

Have you ever noticed that when you are in a bad mood, anything that goes wrong can completely unnerve you? And when you are in a good mood it's harder to knock you off balance? These aren't accidents. It is evidence that the frustrating situation is not completely responsible for your feelings. There are other variables. Consider how a hundred people could go through the same situation, and each of them will handle it differently. The variance is the result of how we think about our situations, which is a product of our experiences, our personalities and our coping skills.

Since our thoughts tend to be automatic, we cannot always prevent negative thoughts from popping into our heads. But we *can* challenge them. As we do this, we get better and better at creating a peaceful and joyful mind.

Very often the most toxic thoughts we have are those about ourselves. Many of my clients put themselves down on a regular basis. They beat themselves up over how they look, what they eat, how messy their homes are or their lack of financial success. They judge their parenting, convinced that they are damaging their children. These are all good people—good parents, good friends, and good neighbors. They set such high standards for themselves that they often fall short. Self-criticism is the worst kind of toxic mind. It eats away at your self-worth and zaps your joy. It is hard to be joyful when you are under attack all the time.

Some of the categories of **toxic mind** include:

- **Awfulizing** - Turning little problems into big problems. ("It's terrible that my husband forgot to unload the dishwasher as he promised." "My life is a disaster.")

- **Always/Never -** Using extreme language that creates more intense feelings. ("You never listen to me." "I always screw up")

- **Mind Reading** - Assuming you or others have, or should have, the ability to read minds- ("I know you think that I look ugly." "He should have known that I wanted to leave early." "Everyone thinks I'm stupid.")

- **Comparison/Perfectionism** - Comparing yourself, or others, to someone else, and coming up short. ("My house will never look as good as Emma's." "I only got a 92 on my math test, but John got a 96." "Why do my kids have to be so difficult? Ben and Ann don't have the problems we have." "I'll never be as skinny as Maya.")

- **Hateful Talk –** Speaking about the things that bother you in an extreme way. ("I hate this show." "I hate Joe." "I hate it when I lose my keys.")

- **Negative Lens** - Focusing on the negative in any situation. ("We saw two shows, but the theaters were so crowded." "I only came in second place." "I won a brand new phone, but now I have to figure out how to use it.")

The problem with all of these bad habits is that they are unnecessarily extreme. As we learn to recognize self-defeating thought patterns, we can begin to replace them with more appropriate thoughts that feel better. We can learn to *downgrade* the *intensity* of our negative thoughts, which will allow us to feel calmer and happier.

Try these instead:

- "It's annoying that my husband forgot to unload the dishwasher."
- "My life has its ups and downs."
- "I don't like it when you don't listen to me."

- "I made a mistake, but I will get it right next time."
- "I can't be sure what you think of me. I guess I'm feeling unattractive."
- "I wanted to leave early; next time I'll make sure I tell you."
- "I'm embarrassed that I didn't know the answer, but that can happen to anybody."
- "I work hard and don't always have time to clean. I need to cut myself some slack."
- "A 92 is really good. I don't need to compare myself to anyone else."
- "My kids are just kids, and I love them. I can never know for sure what other people are dealing with."
- "My favorite feature is my eyes."
- "Can we watch something else?"
- "I'd rather not spend too much time with Joe."
- "It's frustrating when I lose my keys."
- "The shows were fantastic, and the crowds had such great energy."
- "I'm so proud that I placed with a silver medal."
- "I won a brand new phone! I'm excited to figure out all of the features."

These phrases will leave you feeling much better than the toxic examples listed earlier. When you choose to focus on the positive in any given situation and direct less attention to the unpleasant aspects, you open the door to more joy.

Let your feelings guide you. If you consistently feel bad with certain people and good with others, follow the joy. Spend more time with the people you enjoy. The same goes for the information you receive and the thoughts you think. Spend more time with "good feeling thoughts" and less time with "bad feeling thoughts." As we gravitate away from toxic people and information and manage our toxic mind, we will naturally begin to gravitate towards more joyful experiences. Imagine your feelings as a compass, always headed in the direction of joy.

Joyful Action Steps: Avoid Negativity

1. Limit time with the negative people in your life. You don't have to block or unfriend negative people on Facebook, but you can unfollow them, so their negativity stops showing up in your newsfeed. Limit time with negative friends/family that spend time constantly complaining or criticizing. As you build in more time for the people who make you feel good, you will naturally have less time to spend with the people who steal your joy.

2. Limit your time reading articles that upset you. You can stay informed without drowning yourself in negativity. Read the information that is important and that you can take active steps towards improving. When we feel we can do something about what's going on in the country or the world, we feel better.

3. Stop watching depressing TV shows. If you spend your time watching fictional or even real people leading miserable lives, what does that do for you? Despite the entertainment value, this is not helping you to feel more joyful. Reconsider how you spend your time.

4. Learn how to manage your **Toxic Mind** by replacing extreme thinking with more appropriate, better-feeling thoughts. Let go of the need to use *awfulizing*, *always/never*, *mind reading*, *comparison*, *hateful talk*, and *negative lens* thoughts

Love

"Success is not the key to happiness. Happiness is the key to success. If you love what you are doing, you will be successful."

— *Albert Schweitzer*

Part of the problem with focusing on things that upset us or irritate us is that we ignore the things we love in the process. Remember the man who documented all of the things his wife did that annoyed him?

Again, love and gratitude are connected. If we take the time to focus on the people and the things we love, we appreciate them in the process. So it's a double positive! And back to the Law of Attraction, if we get more of what we focus on, then it makes sense to focus on what we love. So as you journal (journaling is a great tool to stay on track) write a list of the things you love, the people you love and the places you love.

Take an inventory of your life. Do you include the things you love in your daily life? If not, it's time to make a change. If you love massages but can't remember the last time you went for one, make an appointment to get one. If you always have an amazing time when you get together with an old friend, and you haven't seen her or him in a year, put something on the calendar.

The point is that you should surround yourself with things you love, spend time with people you love, visit places you love, and do things you love to do. These things may seem so obvious, yet we often forget about simple self-care as we just move habitually from day to day.

In her book, *The Power*, Rhonda Byrne talks about the power of love and encourages us to focus on this wonderful power. I read the book on a flight to Aruba. She discussed the idea of focusing your energy on something you love and watching it materialize, as a sort of 'test' of the power of love. While on vacation, we went to a butterfly farm. We had arrived before it opened, so I was standing outside admiring the beautiful flowers. I said to my family that I would love to see a hummingbird. (I love hummingbirds, but rarely see them). I talked about how it would be so nice to see one because I get so excited when I do. Within a minute, a hummingbird flew down to a flower on a branch right in front of me. It hovered for a few seconds then flew away. I was thrilled!

When the butterfly farm opened, the woman apologized for being late. I told her it was fine since I even got to see a hummingbird while I waited. She was surprised. She said, "We get so excited when we see them too because we rarely do!" Three days later we returned to the butterfly farm, and while I stood outside, I said, "I'd love to see that hummingbird again." No sooner were the words out of my mouth than the hummingbird flew right in front of me and then flew away. The power of love in action!

I talk to my clients about the things they love and ask them to put a list together. When I have a client who is depressed, I try to encourage her to surround herself with things she loves, and I try to help her find things to do that she enjoys. You would be amazed how many people are completely unaware of their likes. Even clients who aren't specifically depressed are often stumped by this question.

So that becomes the work. I ask my clients to be a detective for themselves and to search for things they like. As they notice something that brings a smile to their face, I have them jot it down on a list in their phones. I ask them to list foods they like and pictures they are drawn to on social media. A lot of my younger clients use Instagram or Tumbler. I encourage them to look for the common threads. What things do you have a lot of pictures of? Is it waterfalls or beaches? Sunsets or baby animals? All of these?

If you think these are things that you can't have in your life, think again. If you have lots of pictures of exotic places and you don't think you'll ever get there, you are being self-defeating. Who says you can't get there eventually? And in the meantime, if you are attracted to exotic waterfalls, there may be beautiful waterfalls within driving distance. Make a plan to see some of them. Just because you can't get to Fiji today doesn't mean you can't take a trip to a waterfall nearby this weekend. If you like pictures of sunsets, go outside and watch one live and in person. If you love baby animals, visit a nearby farm or go to an adoption event at a local pet store to look at the puppies and kittens. Bring the things you love to you. Don't deprive yourself of all of the things that make you happy.

I love being near the water. Living on Long Island there is water all around me. It's funny, but many years ago I nearly forget that I had someplace I loved so close to me. I never made time to visit the water. But now I remember that visiting the water during good times highlights my good mood, and during bad times offers comfort and hope. I now make it a habit of going for walks by the nearby pond on a regular basis and visiting the docks or the beach often. I am so grateful these places I love are so accessible to me.

As I mentioned earlier, when I am going through a difficult time with someone that I care about, I often make lists of the qualities about him or her that I love. Even if, at the moment, they are irritating me, I remember the many things I love about them. When I do this, I feel so much better. In my home, I have lots of pictures of my children when they were little. When I am dealing with a snarky remark or a teenage attitude, I like to look at their baby pictures and remember the incredible love that I felt when they were so little. That love is, of course, always there but sometimes I need a reminder of how cute and innocent they once were.

The focus away from love is never more apparent to me than when I work with couples. Couples usually enter therapy after years of misery and negative focus. I find this interesting because very often each person can see their partner's contribution to the negativity but they don't always recognize it in their own actions.

Many times, as I try to take the session in a more positive direction, it becomes clear that they don't *want* to go there. They want to focus on *their* misery. They need it to be validated and acknowledged. One of the first things I learned in social work school was to "start where the client is." So I allow them each to vent, and I help them to see the other's perspective. Then I try to help them remember the qualities that they love in their partner.

I enjoy hearing the stories about how couples met, how they fell in love, and the qualities that they admired in each other. I love to see them laugh as they recall funny moments, and cry as they recall difficult times that they shared.

They begin to reconnect as they remember who they are and who they've been as a couple. Somewhere along the way, they forgot how to focus on the love they had for each other. Somewhere between the dirty dishes, dirty diapers, and money struggles, their focus moved from love and joy to stress and pain.

It takes a conscious effort to stay in the focus of love. And it takes even more of an effort to go back to that focus when you've been away so long. But it is worth it? Try to focus your energy in the direction of love. See how good it feels.

Joyful Action Steps: Love

1. Make a list of the people with whom you love to spend time.

2. For the people closest to you, make a list of all the qualities you love about them. Refer to this list when you are struggling with them.

3. Make a list of the places you love to visit. It can include general places like "the beach" or "the woods, " and it can also include specific places such as, "Disney World" or "Louis and Aisha's cabin in Maine."

4. Make a list of your favorite foods.

5. Make a list of your favorite colors.

6. Make a list of the things you love to do.

7. Make a list of things you love to see (Ex. Hummingbirds, flowers blooming in the spring, rainbows, sunsets, sunrises, stars, puppies, kittens, babies, etc.).

8. Refer to these lists often, and consider how you can add more of these things to your life. Choose several items, and find a way to add these joy-giving things into your everyday life

Mindful Wonder

"Never say there is nothing beautiful in the world anymore. There is always something to make you wonder in the shape of a tree, the trembling of a leaf."

— *Albert Schweitzer*

Mindfulness is the practice of being present in the moment. It is about being fully aware of where you are, and how you feel. Children are naturally mindful. Watch a child playing with his toys, building with blocks, following a butterfly or catching fireflies. Young Children live their lives in a state of endless wonder. They are filled with curiosity and excitement about their environment. We often forget how to be that way as we get older. We get caught up in multi-tasking and trying to get so much done in so little time. We forget to stop and smell the proverbial roses.

Living in mindful wonder, to me, is about being in awe of the world in which we live. My kids have told me that I am like a seven-year-old at times because I get so genuinely excited about little things. They laugh at my excitement over seeing a hummingbird or a rainbow. I get giddy when I see baby animals (or any animals for that matter), but I wouldn't have it any other way. I never want to take the beauty around me for granted. I never want to lose a sense of wonder at the gifts that nature or the universe provides. It brings so much joy to appreciate these things actively.

Despite their amusement at my excitement, I can see that my children also feel the same way. On a road trip with my daughter last year we were driving into the sunset. It was an incredible sunset that lasted for over an hour. As we drove, we were both "oohing" and "ahhing" over the spectacular and vibrant colors. We were amazed at how they kept changing and getting more and more breathtaking. It was a very special moment to share together. My daughter frequently goes to the beach to watch the sunset, and she has often traveled an hour and a half to watch the sunrise in Montauk (at the tip of Long Island). She is no stranger to mindful wonder.

My husband and I share this appreciation of moments of mindful wonder, and we have both tried to instill it in our children. One time when we were staying at my brother and sister-in-law's house on Lake George, we woke our children up and carried them out to the dock during a meteor shower. We sat in Adirondack chairs with blankets, cuddled up to watch the nighttime show. We've driven to nearby docks to watch lightning storms across the Long Island Sound. We often sit by the window to watch snowstorms and rainstorms. We sat in our driveway with hot chocolate and popcorn watching a recent lunar eclipse through a telescope. We don't like to pass up these special once in a lifetime moments.

I've noticed that people that take the time to stop and smell the roses, or admire a sunset, or look at the moon, tend to be happier, at least at that moment. As far as science goes, research has shown that walking in the woods can decrease your level of stress, and being near the water can reduce anxiety and depression. But I don't need a scientist to tell me that being in nature is *good* for me. Being in nature is healing, but appreciating nature is even more so.

When you take the time to notice the little things in your life, it can bring a sense of peace that is so needed to maintain a joyful life. It isn't the big things in life that bring us pure joy. It is the little things every day that help us live joyfully. Big moments make us happy. But the feeling often passes after the moment is over. Joy is a more powerful feeling that goes deeper. Watch a mother or father with their baby. Watch as they play with their baby's tiny toes and look into their eyes. Yes, this is love, but it is also *wonder* or *awe*. They are in a moment of *mindful wonder*, fully present with their baby. Pet owners feel the same way about their adorable fur babies. They watch them as they sleep and are in love with their ears and paws. They just can't believe how lucky they are to have something so precious. There is a feeling of amazement. That is what you want to bring to your life every day.

In addition to the daily moments of mindful wonder, when my husband and I go on vacation with the family, we always love to plan something that we have never done. We love going seal, dolphin or whale watching. The awe we have felt seeing dozens of whales in the ocean right next to us was incredible for all of us. We were astounded. We've taken a bioluminescent bay canoe tour in Puerto Rico (there are organisms in the water that give off a burst of bright blue light when touched or moved). It was completely magical. We also visited a rainforest on that same trip. We've done an adventure course in the trees in The Adirondacks. Wherever we go, we look for experiences that are unique to that place.

I recently had the opportunity to go to Australia to visit my daughter who was studying there. One day, we visited a beach where little penguins came out of the rocky shore at sunset. It was incredible to see them in their natural habitat just inches away from us. I was so excited the feeling lasted for days and still returns whenever I look at a picture or recall it in my mind. That was a moment of true wonder, and I was so happy to share it with my daughter and her friends.

These moments don't always have to be in a natural environment. My son is a guitar player and loves music. His first concert, when he was about ten years old, was Paul McCartney at Citi Field. I was starstruck being at a concert of an actual Beatle! My son didn't understand the enormity of it until later, but he did become a huge Beatles fan. In the past several years he has seen many of his idols in concert, including Eric Clapton, Eddie Van Halen, Jeff Beck, and Dweezil Zappa. He has experienced the wonder and awe of these moments, and I was in awe seeing him completely immersed in the experience of seeing his idols and inspirations performing live.

My husband and I took our son to Woodstock last summer. It was all about his love of music. We visited Bethel where the actual Woodstock festival took place, and we stood on the site of the stage where so many legends once stood. We also visited the "Big Pink House" where Bob Dylan and The Band created some of their most iconic music. It was a very simple trip but full of inspiration and wonder.

I encourage everyone to create "wonder-filled" experiences to enjoy. Seek out opportunities to feel a sense of wonder or awe in your everyday life. Create special moments around your personal interests. These moments help to create your life of joy.

Joyful Action Steps: Mindful Wonder

1. Think about moments in your life when you were in a state of mindful wonder. Maybe when your child was born, when you saw a hero of yours in real life, when you watched a beautiful sunset. Consider these moments. Many may be on your lists from the previous exercise.

2. Consider ways to experience mindful wonder during a normal day. Watch squirrels playing outside and consider that they are living beings enjoying a joyful life. Watch a butterfly and think about the transformation that it has gone through to become the beautiful creature it is. Play with a baby and think about the miracle of life. Find as many ways as you can to appreciate and revel in mindful wonder.

3. Plan wonder-filled experiences such as getting up early to watch a sunrise, catching a meteor shower, or visiting a butterfly house. If you are planning a trip, look for ways to build new experiences into the trip.

4. In the words of EB White, "Always be on the lookout for the presence of wonder."

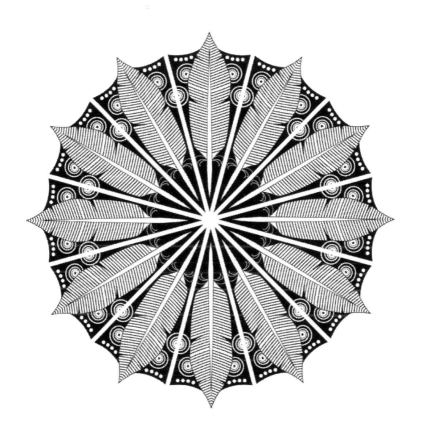

From Worry to Hope

"Hope is like the sun, which, as we journey toward it, casts the shadow of our burden behind us."

— Samuel Smiles

Letting Go of Fear and Worry

Fear is a joy killer. It keeps us from doing things that we would enjoy, and it keeps us from achieving all we can. I am no stranger to fear. Fear has kept me from pursuing some of my dreams, and it has kept me in a state of worry more times than I would like to admit.

Fear and worry are best friends. They go everywhere together. Fear can be debilitating. It can keep people from experiencing any joy at all. Fear of failure; fear and worry about the well-being of our children, our parents or partners; fear about the state of the country or the world; these fears can all be overwhelming at times.

Most of the things we fear are completely outside of our control. That is the hardest part of all. The truth is we will do everything we can to keep our loved ones happy and healthy; we will work hard, so we don't fail; we will speak up about issues in the world that are important to us. But the things we have no control over are the things we tend to fear the most. So what can we do to deal with our fear and our worry? How do we manage those feelings?

Hope

The antidote to fear is hope. That's right…the antidote to fear and worry is very simply *hope*. Hope can take the fear away.

Hope is the tiny spark that things might not turn out all bad. It is the little voice that says, "Maybe it will be okay." Fear cannot reside where hope lives. I have seen the moment when hope shows up for my clients many times. I am always looking for it. It is the moment when I *know* change will occur. It isn't always spoken, but I can see it. I can *feel* it. It is when a client who is convinced she will never find love after a relationship ends, has the fleeting thought, "Maybe I will." It's when the couple that is constantly fighting finds a moment of clarity and understanding of each other.

You can see his tiny thing called "hope." I look for it daily with my clients. I try to help my friends see it when they are feeling lost, and I search for it quietly when I am caught in worry or fear mode myself.

The concept that everything is falling into place is hard to recognize during difficult times. When the walls seem to be crumbling around you, it's hard to have hope for a better future. And yet, time after time, I have seen that this is true.

I recently was reminded of this when thinking about certain people that we had met who turned out to be important in our lives. I thought about the difficult times that led them to us, and how sad it would be if they had never entered our lives. It was through the struggle that we were led to them, or they to us. I hear this all the time, not just about people, but about things that never would have happened without the drama or struggle that came before.

There is an old proverb about a farmer. This farmer had only one horse, and one day the horse ran away. The neighbors came to console him over his terrible loss.

The farmer said, "What makes you think it is so terrible?"

A month later, the horse came home–this time bringing two beautiful wild horses with her. The neighbors became excited at the farmer's good fortune.

The farmer said, "What makes you think this is good fortune?"

Shortly after, the farmer's son was thrown from one of the wild horses and broke his leg. All the neighbors were very distressed. Such bad luck!

The farmer said, "What makes you think it is bad?"

War came, and every non-disabled man was sent into battle. Only the farmer's son, because he had a broken leg, remained.

The point is, we don't always know what is coming, and in the midst of the trials and tribulations of life, we often forget that it is not the end of the road. Many times the good that comes to us can only come about as a result of the struggles we've suffered before.

Everything can change in a day. The day before you meet the love of your life can be an ordinary day, as can the day before you win the lottery. I have had clients that were miserable because they thought there was no one on Earth who would love them, and the next time I saw them they were beaming because they met that special someone. I've had clients who were frustrated with their finances, and then they landed a big job with a substantial increase in salary. They couldn't predict the moment it would happen.

The day before something wonderful occurs is often just another day; maybe even a bad day. So think how happy we would be if we knew something incredible was about to happen? It *is*, but you just don't know when.

Earlier, I discussed the power of visualization. When worry hijacks your mind, you can use the power of visualization to free yourself. If you can remember the story above, you can remind yourself that you have no way of knowing what good is coming. So have fun imagining the best possible outcome.

As I mentioned earlier, athletes have been using the power of visualization forever. If you check any successful team or athlete before a big event, you will most likely find them visualizing success. They picture themselves scoring a goal, making a basket or getting a run. They picture success. Visualizing failure is not how you win a game or land a job, or overcome an illness.

"Use your imagination until your big dream feels so familiar that its manifestation is the next logical step." – Abraham-Hicks

Many of my clients have tried this with great success. One client was very worried about her child's health. She was taking him for a test and was fearful about the results. I encouraged her to imagine only the outcome she was hoping for. I told her to picture herself hearing the good news and to imagine the sense of relief she would feel. I wanted her to focus on hope, not on worry. Since worrying wouldn't make it better, if she could live in a state of hope she would certainly feel better leading up to the test.

She did a beautiful job imagining the best outcome, and she helped herself through. She still had some anxiety, but she consciously focused on the outcome she desired. The test went well, and the outcome was as hoped for! Whether or not you believe that the Law of Attraction helped her to create this outcome, there is certainly no denying that hope *feels* better than worry.

So the next time you are worried or fearful, take some time to imagine the outcome you *hope* for, not the outcome you *fear*. Imagine the result you want in as much detail as you possibly can. Feel the feelings of your reaction to the good news or the success you are seeking. Get swept up in the feelings. Imagine the best. Get carried away with hope!

Look for Signs of Hope from the Universe

When you are worried, or anxious, or sad, it helps to know that things will get better. But sometimes you just need a sign, something tangible to say, "There's a light at the end of the tunnel."

When I, or someone I love, is struggling I am always grateful for, what I consider to be, signs from the universe that everything will be okay. Some of the signs that I have seen include things like: a cloud, a leaf or rock shaped like a heart; a feather; a coin; etc. It could be virtually anything meaningful to *you*. I have a friend who finds hearts everywhere—in nature, in food, even in garbage. These 'signs' offer comfort to her and those with whom she shares her stories. Another friend of mine finds nickels every time she is going through a struggle. She sees them as a gift from a loved one who has passed on.

It doesn't matter how you think they show up or what the sign even is. The point is to trust in these signs as a way to comfort you through difficult times.

One day, when I was feeling worried about a loved one, I was walking by the pond, and I just thought softly to myself, "I need a sign that things will be okay." Within seconds, I saw a heart shaped stone on the path. As I continued, I saw broken concrete holes, leaves and a cloud in the shape of a heart. I walked this path every day and never noticed any of these things. But when I needed a sign, they were there. You can call it coincidence or whatever you want; it doesn't matter. At that moment I felt better. I felt comforted. And above all else, I had *HOPE*! The people in my life, who accept signs from whatever they believe to be providing them, understand the power of hope and how important it is to soothe our worries and fears.

Joyful Action Steps: From Worry to Hope

1. Fold a piece of paper in half vertically.

2. Label one side "important" and the other side "unimportant."

3. Make a list of things you are worried about and write each item on the appropriate side of the page.

4. Cross off the side marked "unimportant." You have just cut your worries in half. After all, there's no point in worrying about things that aren't important.

5. Look at the list. Is there anything that is out of your control that you may be able to take some control over? If you are worried about the environment, is there something that you may be able to do to advocate or get involved in some way?

6. Now review what remains on the list. Cross off anything that you have no control over.

7. What are left are your concerns. These are things that are both important to you and within your control. You can now take action in whatever way is possible. If you are concerned about an aging parent, call and check in on them. If you are concerned about the environment, join an environmental group. If you are concerned about your health, begin an exercise program, meet with a nutritionist or

schedule an appointment with your doctor. If you are concerned about how a child is doing at school, schedule an appointment with their teacher. You get the idea. When things are unimportant, and we waste our time and energy on them, we feel depleted. Let them go. We can also spend a great deal of time worrying about things outside of our control. We feel powerless. At that point, we can decide if there is something we can do to help us feel like we are at least doing our part in making it better. We begin to gain some control. If there is truly nothing you can do, try to let it go. Focus your energy on the things that are most important to you and that you can do something about.

8. For those worries that are very important that feel out of your control, try to develop a sense of hope that things will be okay. Even if it is not the way, we wish for it to be, recognize that whatever happens, you'll handle it.

9. Every day, while showering, as you wash your body, imagine that you are washing away all of your worries and fears. Imagine that the strength of the water is removing all of your worries and any negative feelings that are sticking to you. Watch as they go down the drain along with the soap. It is a very powerful exercise that can leave you feeling calmer and more at ease. Remember the power of visualization.

10. Look for the gift in your struggles, if not during the struggle, then by reflecting on it afterward. If we can remember this during our struggles, it can even lighten your heart and ease your mind a little bit.

11. Look for "signs from the universe" that provide you with a sense of hope. Whatever signs are meaningful to you are perfect. Heart-shaped items, feathers, butterflies, coins, shooting stars, a certain type of bird or flower, etc. Let these signs offer you hope that things will get better.

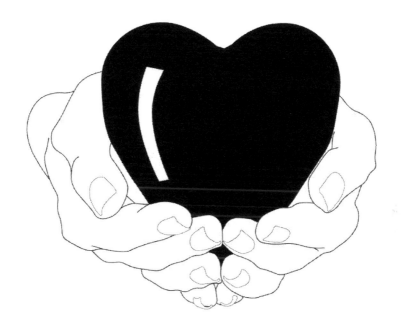

Compassion

"If you want others to be happy, practice compassion. If you want to be happy, practice compassion."

— *Dalai Lama*

What does compassion have to do with joy? It has *everything* to do with it. Compassion wants others to be free from suffering. The opposites of compassion are hatred, indifference, and coldness. Angry, hateful people are not happy. They are not joyful. The ability to wish others well, and free from suffering, opens your heart in ways that focusing on yourself just can't.

Anxiety and depression are very self-focused. It is healthy to focus on yourself; to address your needs and what is important in your life. However, anxiety and depression involve a lack of self-compassion. The focus is on what is wrong with you and your life. They both involve forms of self-criticism. When you are so focused on everything that's wrong with you, it is hard to feel joyful.

When you show compassion for another person or animal, you feel good. When you are feeling good, helping others amplifies your joy. When you are struggling at any time in your life, the ability to help another can bring joy to you, as the helper, as well as to the person you help.

Think about a time you may have been feeling down, and then a friend called you because they needed to talk. As you listened and supported them, your bad feelings probably passed. As you focused on their suffering and making them feel better, you probably started to feel better yourself. Your compassion pulled you out of yourself, a great thing to do if you are anxious or upset.

Helping is Healing, which is why I often "prescribe" volunteer work to clients who are depressed or anxious. Helping others, particularly others who have it worse than you, can make you feel good and can give you the added bonus of perspective. You begin to appreciate your own situation.

Giving of yourself to others, through your time, money or other gifts, increases your level of joy. In an experiment published in *Science* by Michael Norton, a Harvard Business School professor, participants received a sum of money. Half of the participants were told to spend the money on themselves, and the other half were told to spend the money on others. At the end of the study, participants that had spent money on others felt significantly happier than those that had spent money on themselves. Compassion in action sparks joy.

There is so much research right now that supports the notion that we are all connected. When we treat others with compassion or connect with them in that way, we experience higher levels of happiness.

When we are willing to see another's suffering and try to understand how they may feel, compassion is the natural result. When I would go to New York City from time to time, usually for a show or dinner, my heart would ache when I saw homeless men, women (some pregnant), and children sitting on the street while people rushed by without looking. It's easier not to look, but I couldn't look away. I felt like I needed them to know that I saw them. They weren't invisible. Giving them money just didn't seem like enough. During the holidays, a couple of years ago, my family and I bought blankets and put bags together with various items that people might need. We thought about what they are dealing with and what could be helpful and included those items in the bags such as lotions, gloves, socks, hand and foot warmers, toothpaste and toothbrushes, lip balm, etc. We also thought about how sad it must be to see everyone around them shopping and celebrating during the holiday season while they have so little. We decided to include in each package homemade cookies, candy canes, and a card with a personal note stating that they are cared for.

As my family and I gave out the bags and blankets, we talked to the people and showed care and concern for them. We listened to them. We looked them in the eyes. We were all so incredibly moved by the many reactions we witnessed. They were all so appreciative. Sadly, we ran out of blankets and bags. There were too many homeless people to help. But we all felt good about what we did. It didn't cost a fortune. It took a little bit of time. But it made a difference to them and *us*. It felt like the right thing to do. It felt more meaningful than just giving each other presents. Showing compassion improves your life.

Compassion is the natural result of hearing or trying to understand someone's story. When I first became a social worker, I was working in an Employee Assistance Program in a hospital. My job was to counsel employees and to refer many of them for treatment. One day

I received a mandated referral for a man who abused his girlfriend. He needed a referral to an abusers program. I did not want this case. I did not want to sit in the same room with this man. I didn't even really want to help him. But I had no choice.

When he came in, I felt scared. He was very large and very menacing. I was inexperienced and young, and I was frightened and intimidated by his presence. I was disgusted by what he did. But he was there for help, so I met with him. As he spoke about the abuse he inflicted on his girlfriend, I cringed inside. He talked about himself and his fear of being alone. He showed me his vulnerability. He cried. I saw the pain in his eyes. He spoke about how he didn't want her to leave him. He spoke about his childhood of being abused and where his fears began. His story was heartbreaking. It was terrifying. I saw the frightened child in him.

Before meeting him I didn't think it would have been possible, but sitting there in that office, I felt compassion for this man. I detested what he had done. But once I heard his story, I felt for him and his struggle. I wanted to help him, not just for him, but for his girlfriend and for any children he may have some day in the future. He wanted help. He didn't want to be the way he was. Compassion came when I didn't look away. It came when I listened. I didn't want it or expect it, but it came.

That client made me a better person and a better therapist. As a psychotherapist, I hear people's stories. The stories about what they've done, how they feel and who they think they are. I hear about their pain and their shame. It is a very special job, sitting with people's stories. I know it is my job to listen without judgment. Compassion is a gift that I give them as they give me the gift of their stories.

Self-Compassion

Compassion, however, must start with us. As I mentioned earlier, if we do not show ourselves compassion, we are likely to feel anxious or depressed. Self-compassion is the ability to be kind to yourself, to have an inner dialogue that is supportive and non-critical. Self-compassion allows you to be imperfect without feeling like a failure. Self-compassion recognizes your struggles and supports you just like a good friend would do.

Some people are much better at being compassionate towards others than they are towards themselves. I have been guilty of this myself. But *you* must be included in the circle of compassion. Compassion allows you to recognize that we are all connected, and when you see that, you want everyone to be free from suffering, yourself included.

The first step toward developing self-compassion is recognizing the harsh ways we speak to ourselves. Being aware of how we criticize ourselves allows us to challenge the negative self-talk. It's helpful to write down some of the things you say to yourself that are unkind, and then consider how you would support someone else who spoke that way about themselves. Write down these soothing words and recall them when you catch yourself in a cycle of negative self-talk. You deserve as much compassion as anyone else. If you struggle with this, in particular, I encourage you to find a supportive therapist to help you. It is critical to your happiness.

When compassion is missing for others, or ourselves, we allow judgment to creep in. A lack of compassion is evident when we are harsh, critical or judgmental. When you notice that you are feeling that way it's time to amp up your compassion. When we are critical or judgmental of others, we are not compassionate towards them, and most likely not towards ourselves as well. Tune into your feelings at those times, and see if you can find it in your heart to be more supportive and compassionate to the target of your judgment. Doing so will alleviate those harsh feelings, and allow more joy to enter your life. Remember that when you are in a critical or judgmental state, you are not in alignment with joy.

My dad was an extremely kind and compassionate man. One of his life mottos was, "If you don't have anything nice to say, don't say anything at all." He lived by those words. I can honestly say that I can't remember a time when he spoke unkindly about anyone. I remember one time when I was a young teenager gossiping on the phone with a friend; he shook his head and reminded me of those words. It was a time in my life when I didn't feel the best about myself, to say the least. I continue to work on this ongoing challenge.

When I find myself being critical or judgmental, if I take a closer look, I often notice that I am being hard on myself which spilled over into being critical of others. As I focus on compassion, for others, and myself, I notice how much better I feel. My clients have also benefited from understanding the importance of compassion. As they learn to be more compassionate with themselves, it often follows that they are more compassionate with others.

A Note on Compassion Fatigue

There are many people who are so compassionate that they become consumed by the sadness in others. They are so empathic that they feel intensely for others' suffering, which can lead to compassion fatigue. People in helping professions can be at risk for compassion fatigue because the work they do requires them to be compassionate for others, and they are likely to be naturally empathic.

Some of the signs of compassion fatigue include: feeling burned out, feeling numb, difficulty sleeping, weight loss, headaches, feeling chronically exhausted both emotionally and physically.

It is critical for those who find themselves being overwhelmed by their compassion for others to practice extra self-care. Spending time in nature, meditation, eating well, getting exercise and speaking with a therapist can all be beneficial for those suffering from compassion fatigue.

If you feel you are suffering from compassion fatigue, you should also be sure to engage in light, fun activities in your free time to balance your compassionate and heavy-hearted work. Avoid sad movies or intense TV shows, take time off from work when you can, and take breaks during the day.

Laughter is a powerful tool in coping with compassion fatigue. Spend time with people who make you laugh, listen to comedy radio, and watch funny movies or TV shows. Laughter will help you heal. It releases endorphins, lowers stress hormones and promotes a feeling of well-being. Do not allow yourself to feel guilty for having fun. Keeping yourself miserable will not lessen the suffering of others. You do not have to be a martyr. In fact, the good feelings you create will be healing to others as well.

Allow yourself to be joyful by practicing what you learn in this book. As you fill yourself with joy, you will bring healing to others as you radiate joyful energy for others to experience. Remember, what you give to yourself, you also give to others.

Joyful Action Steps: Compassion

Metta Meditation (Loving Kindness)

This meditation allows you to connect with yourself and others. It helps you let go of resentment and find forgiveness. In the meditation, you will be sending love to yourself and others. You always start with yourself because you can't give what you don't have. Many people experience shifts in relationships after doing the Metta.

We are all made up of energy, and as we send out the energy of love, it can return to us in surprising ways. You may find, after doing this meditation with sincerity, that you begin to care about the person you were indifferent to. The relationship with the person you were angry with may shift, if not externally, then perhaps in your mind. You may be able to let go of resentments that have affected you. And your relationship with the person you care about may grow and deepen.

Start by sitting comfortably with your eyes closed. Imagine what you wish for in your life. We are going to focus on being joyful, being healthy and strong, and our lives being full of peace. You can choose any three or four things you'd like.

You are going to imagine a ball of white light circling in your heart—the light of love.

Start by directing the phrases to yourself.

- "May I be joyful."
- "May I be healthy and strong."
- "May my life be full of peace."

Now you will be sending love to others. As you imagine this with each person or people, imagine the light of love spreading from your heart to theirs. As you speak the words, feel the love that you are sending. Remember that they are just like you. They are people who want the same things in life that you do.

Next, you will direct the Metta towards someone you feel thankful for, someone who has helped you, or someone you love. Once you have the picture of that person in your mind, imagine a swirling white light spreading from your heart to his or hers. Now send the Metta.

- "May you be joyful."
- "May you be healthy and strong."
- "May your life be full of peace."

Now visualize someone you feel neutral about. Someone you don't know well, or feel neither positively or negatively about. Imagine the white light moving to the person's heart.

- "May you be joyful."
- "May you be healthy and strong."
- "May your life be full of peace."

Next, visualize someone you are having a hard time with or someone you don't like. This can be hard to do but try to remember that that person wants the same basic things in life that you do. What we send out returns to us. Imagine the white light moving from your heart to his or hers. And direct the Metta to him or her.

- "May you be joyful."
- "May you be healthy and strong."
- "May your life be full of peace."

Finally, let's direct it to everyone in the universe. Imagine the white light spreading from your heart across the universe.

- "May all beings everywhere be joyful."
- "May all beings everywhere be healthy and strong."
- "May all beings everywhere be full of peace."

Repeat this meditation daily. It doesn't take long, but it can have a profound effect on your life.

Forgiveness

"We must develop and maintain the capacity to forgive. He who is devoid of the power to forgive is devoid of the power to love. There is some good in the worst of us and some evil in the best of us. When we discover this, we are less prone to hate our enemies."

— *Martin Luther King, Jr.*

Forgiveness is critical in the creation of joy. When we do not forgive, we are harboring resentments and anger. Learning to forgive is an act of love for *you*. We have all heard that we don't forgive someone for them; we forgive for us. Holding onto grudges towards another will only tear you apart bit by bit.

Dr. Fred Luskin of the Stanford University Forgiveness Project defines forgiveness as "the feeling of peace that emerges as you take your hurt less personally, take responsibility for how you feel, and become a hero instead of a victim in the story that you tell. Forgiveness is the experience of peacefulness in the present moment."

I love this definition of forgiveness for a few reasons. First, it states that we need to take responsibility for how we feel. We are not responsible for what others do to us, but we *can* take responsibility for our reaction and for how we let it affect us.

Second, I love the concept of being a hero rather than a victim. People who practice forgiveness are heroes. There is a story that comes to mind of a woman who was critically injured many years ago when a teenager threw a frozen turkey through her windshield. It crushed nearly every bone in her face. This incident happened near my home. The community was shocked and upset by this incident. This woman, Victoria Ruvolo, endured endless surgeries and horrible pain. However, at the hearing for the young man who did this to her, she pleaded for his leniency. She forgave him. In an interview with the *Daily News* she stated, "If I hadn't let go of that anger, I'd be consumed by this need for revenge. Forgiving him helps me move on."

She didn't ask to be a hero. She didn't want this horrible experience, but in many ways, it came to define the person that she is. She has woven this into her life, and now she serves as an inspiration to others.

Throughout our lives, we are going to be hurt, and we are going to inflict some hurt too. We aren't going to get out of this life completely unscathed. People are imperfect and will do things that affect others in negative ways. It is hard to be on the receiving end of these hurts. It is also hard to know you've hurt another. We want to know that we will be forgiven for what we've done wrong. If we don't learn how to forgive others and ourselves, we will have a very hard time being happy or joyful.

We all have our own stories of hurt that we can tell. The pain can seem as fresh as if it just happened, even if it was many years ago. We hold onto these stories and the hurt and resentment that go along with them. They can become part of our identity and even affect our other relationships.

Learning to let go is an important step toward being a more joyful person. Forgiveness does not necessarily mean reconciling with someone who has wronged you. They don't even have to know about your forgiveness if you don't want to contact the person.

When we forgive, we make a decision not to let our feelings of anger dominate our thoughts. We choose to accept that whatever happened, happened. We can try to understand where the person was in their life that caused them to hurt us. In this way, we develop compassion for them. Compassion may be a prerequisite for forgiveness. As we understand the other person, and why they did what they did, we can forgive the wounded part of them that caused us pain. And then we make a decision to let it go—to keep it in the past where it belongs. It is the decision to forgive, which sets us free and allows us to live joyfully.

When Forgiveness Isn't an Option

If you were a victim of severe trauma or abuse, you might struggle with the concept of forgiveness. That is completely understandable. You may not want to forgive, and that is your right. Expecting someone to forgive in these instances may be asking for too much. Your goal is to feel a sense of freedom from your painful feelings; to get to a point where you can take back your power.

Working with a compassionate therapist can help you understand and accept your feelings, and help you to feel empowered again. Forgiveness is not necessary for healing in these situations. Each person has the right to choose to forgive or not. Forgiveness for many is freeing. However, only you know if you are willing or able to forgive—now or ever. It is *always* your choice.

Self-Forgiveness

I would be remiss in talking about forgiveness without discussing self-forgiveness. In my practice and my life, I often see people struggling to forgive themselves. Carrying around guilt and shame will not correct a mistake, nor will it make you a better person. It is crucial to your well-being that you practice self-forgiveness. It is an act of love for yourself, and yes, you deserve it.

Forgiving yourself does not mean that it is okay for you to keep making the same mistakes over and over. It doesn't mean you can be unkind and cruel then all will be forgiven. When you recognize your mistakes, you can come clean and commit to doing better. You release your past because you did the best you could at that time with the skills and resources you had.

When you know better, you can do better. It is up to you to be the person you want to be. Punishing yourself for the rest of your life will not serve you or anyone else for that matter.

Forgiving yourself starts with taking responsibility for your actions. Guilt is an important feeling. It starts out good. It shows you have a conscience and that you have empathy. Guilt is the feeling that says you know you did something or said something you probably shouldn't have. But too many people hold onto guilt and shame, not only for things they've done wrong but even for things outside of their control.

I see this all the time in my practice. I see parents who feel guilty because their children are unhappy or have health issues that are beyond their control. They focus on mistakes they made with their children when they were young, even though their children have grown. I also see adult children of alcoholic parents who feel chronically guilty. These feelings often keep people from living their lives fully. They carry around guilt and shame to punish themselves.

When talking about self-forgiveness, we need to remember that we don't want to release the empathy that evokes the feeling of guilt. That is important to hold onto, to prevent you from becoming cold and uncaring about others in the process of forgiving yourself.

I encourage my clients to learn to forgive themselves for the sake of their well-deserved happiness. Begin to recognize that you are worthy of happiness and *allow* yourself to be happy. Remember how we are seeking to understand others to forgive them? We also need to learn to have empathy for ourselves. Consider why we did what we did. Life isn't always easy, and it can get the best of us at times. We may not always be our best selves.

There are days that I beat myself up for losing patience with my children, or for forgetting something I should have remembered. When I go to bed at night, I sometimes find my thoughts gravitating to all of my mistakes. I have learned to stop myself when I do this, and to say the words, "I forgive myself! Tomorrow I'll do better." This simple action allows me to sleep in peace and start my day fresh in the morning. It is a simple act of self-love that I recommend to my clients as well.

You can also make a list of the good things you do in your life. Are you a thoughtful and caring friend? Do you take good care of your fur babies? Are you a kind neighbor? If you are a parent, consider all the things you do for your children. Do you take care of your partner/spouse? Even if you fall short some of the time, you are certainly stepping up at other times. Why only focus on your shortcomings? Remember the Law of Attraction; what you focus on you get more of. If you focus on your strengths, you will start to show more and more of these good qualities.

Forgiving yourself does not mean it's okay to keep hurting people knowingly. It means you accept your mistakes as mistakes, and you allow yourself to move on. Living with guilt does not correct your mistakes, and it doesn't make the other person feel better. What it does do is keep you from living your life joyfully. And *that* just isn't acceptable.

If you find yourself reliving mistakes you've made (or think you've made), it is time for a little self-forgiveness. I find most people do as well as they can. And the people who are often the hardest on themselves are the same people that give so much of themselves to others.

We will never be perfect! We are human, and mistakes are inevitable. Taking responsibility is hard but forgiving yourself can sometimes be even harder. Don't let guilt and shame stand in the way of your joy.

If this is particularly hard for you, especially if you were a victim of abuse as a child, I encourage you to seek counseling with a caring professional. Your work is to release the shame and guilt of your past, forgive yourself and learn to love yourself. It is important work, and it is well worth the effort!

Forgiveness can be complicated. The act of forgiving can be very healing. However, not everyone is ready to forgive. You get to choose what feels best for you. The goal is to find a sense of peace within you in whatever way you can. Forgiveness may help you with that goal and bring you closer to joy.

The following Buddhist Forgiveness Prayer sums it up nicely.

*If I have harmed anyone in any way either knowingly or
unknowingly through my own confusions
I ask their forgiveness.*

*If anyone has harmed me in any way either knowingly or
unknowingly through their own confusions
I forgive them.*

*And if there is a situation I am not yet ready to forgive
I forgive myself for that.*

*For all the ways that I harm myself, negate, doubt, belittle myself,
judge or be unkind to myself through my own confusions
I forgive myself.*

Joyful Action Steps: Forgiveness

1. Make a list of everyone you are struggling to forgive.

2. Consider each person and why they may have done whatever it is that they did. Truly think about what in their lives may have contributed to the hurt that they inflicted. Doing so does not excuse the behavior; it simply provides some understanding.

3. Picture this person as a wounded child. Imagine that a child who didn't know any better inflicted the wrongdoing upon you.

4. Now imagine yourself giving that child your forgiveness. You can say something like, "I was angry and upset by your behavior. You hurt me terribly. It was wrong, and you need to know that. I will not allow you to hurt me anymore, but I forgive you." You do not have to share this with the person (unless you want to). This is simply in your head, for YOUR benefit. You may even want to write a letter explaining how you feel and stating your forgiveness.

5. Repeat this for everyone that you are struggling to forgive.

6. You can symbolically burn the letters or the list of the people, and imagine that you are releasing any negative attachment that you have to them. This act can be very powerful. It is important to set the intention to release any unforgiveness as you begin.

7. Remember to include yourself in your forgiveness. Learn to focus on your good qualities and allow yourself to be imperfect. You

cannot undo past mistakes, but you can try to do better in the future. This will only happen if you forgive yourself and give yourself permission to be happy.

8.   You can include any and all of these people in the Metta Meditation if you would like.

Connection

*"I knew what my job was; it was to go out
and meet the people and love them."*

— *Princess Diana*

Connection plays a powerful role in joy. When we feel connected to others, we feel more alive, and we experience a greater sense of satisfaction with the relationship.

When working with clients who are depressed, they often express feeling disconnected. That does not mean that they have no one in their lives. Many times they have people in their lives that care about them, but they don't feel that sense of connection that is so satisfying. The lack of connection can, at times, come directly from within. They have not tuned into the people around them in a meaningful way. Being mindful of the people and environment around you can wake you up, in a sense, to experience a more beautiful life.

The Harvard University Grant and Glueck 75-year longitudinal study on happiness (the longest study ever done on the subject) reveals the answer to the question, "What makes people happy?" The answer is, quite simply, social relationships and a feeling of connection to others. The finding is not particularly surprising, but it is significant.

Life can get crazy! We all have so many responsibilities and obligations. It isn't surprising that time flies so fast. We are often shocked that a day, or week, or even a season or year has flown by, and we didn't get an opportunity to see people we care about.

We are a scheduled people. Our children are scheduled. We often don't do something unless it is on our calendar. If we have a toothache, we will fit in an appointment with the dentist. If we get sick, we will often make time for the doctor, but what about our social connections? Do we make time to schedule them in as well? Consider the people you enjoy. Earlier, you made a list of the people you love to spend time with. What if you made it a priority to connect with them, through visits or phone calls?

I know that when I reconnect with a friend I haven't spoken with for a while, I feel happier and brighter. I truly love my friends, and I treasure any time I can have with them, either in person or on the phone.

Our connections to family and friends are critical to our joy. Laughing with people you love and even crying with people you love builds a sense of belonging that is critical to our emotional well-being. I find that sometimes the simplest moments are the most fun. Just having a few hours to talk at a restaurant, or even a quick phone call can be the fuel that I need to boost my mood when I am down, and to elevate it, even more, when I am happy. We need to nurture and cherish these relationships that are so important to us.

Even the people we see every day present opportunities for reconnection. We may see people daily but not necessarily *see* or *connect* with them. When we are busy, we may rush around and go through the motions, but not truly connect. These people require our undivided attention from time to time as well.

When I am working with parents, I often hear of difficulties they have with their children, and what they want their children to do differently. In addition to addressing the behavior issues, I will often recommend ten minutes of connection with each child each night. Ten minutes devoted just to him or her—no phones, no TV—just uninterrupted attention. It doesn't take long, but it has a powerful impact.

When parents devote just ten minutes a day of focused, loving attention, in addition to the other time normally spent, they notice a stronger connection with their child. In two-parent households, I recommend that they each take ten minutes and switch off with the other children. This time allows each parent and child to benefit from the closeness.

From the time we are born, we require constant attention from our caregivers. As we mature, we gain independence, but we never really outgrow the need to be seen and heard. As a therapist, I give undivided, focused attention to my clients. People truly appreciate being heard in this way, and in many ways, I feel it is the most important part of the therapeutic process.

A young woman that I was working with told me that she was telling her mother about therapy. She said, "Susan really *listens* Mom. It's incredible." Her mother dismissed it. My client responded, "No you don't understand; I mean she *really* listens!"

When you truly listen to people, they feel it. They know when you are genuinely trying to understand. Listening is a very powerful thing. It also allows you to feel more connected to the person you are with.

All relationships can benefit from that time as well. Finding little ways to connect throughout the day, or week, are important to a strong partnership. Couples usually devote a lot of time to this early in a relationship, but as time goes by and responsibilities build, the connection part of the relationship may become neglected.

I frequently see this in the couples that come in for therapy. It is what they are looking for in couples therapy. They begin to feel less connected to each other, and they need help re-connecting. In the extreme, the disconnection manifests in infidelity or other types of indiscretions. My work with them is to help them rebuild the connection that they once had. Many times it is communication that needs work. Couples often don't truly hear each other. I see how one person can be talking while the other is hearing something else entirely. I try to teach them how to bridge the gap.

Many couples I've worked with have commented on how surprised they were by just how easy it was to build a stronger connection. They were expecting it to be much harder. Some had been through a variety of trying times and didn't truly go through them together. They each went through the shared experiences separately. Instead of sharing their feelings and experiences, they disconnected. As they began to share with each other and truly listen, they started to understand what their partner was feeling, and they learned the importance of connecting during difficult times as well as happier moments.

Even in our everyday interactions with cashiers, wait staff, postal workers, etc., we have the ability to establish and experience a connection. My children laugh at my husband and me because we tend to talk to everyone. When I treat the people around me with respect and look at them as people, not robots, I feel the connection and so do they. Wherever I go, I find people talking to me and sharing their problems or struggles. They just need an ear for a moment, and I am glad to oblige.

One day, while at lunch with a friend, we had a very annoyed waitress serving us. She was practically throwing the silverware and bread on the table. I could see she was frazzled. So I asked, "You're having a hard day, huh?" She was so grateful for the acknowledgment and responded, "Oh, it's been terrible." She went on to explain about some difficult customers she just had. We sympathized with her and validated her feelings. She immediately turned into the most attentive waitress you could ever imagine. She brought us our food quickly, with a smile and a, "Here you go honey!" She transformed because of a simple moment of connection. And that moment of connection felt good for us as well. When we connect with others, they feel joy, and so do we. It's a win/win.

Joyful Action Steps: Connection

1. Once a week, spend ten to fifteen minutes in the morning on a set day to simply schedule connection time. Put it on your calendar and schedule it to repeat weekly. During those few minutes, contact one or more of the people you want to connect with and schedule some time to either speak with them or get together with them. If you do this weekly, you will be sure to spend more time with people that bring you joy.

2. When you are with someone, *be with them*. When you are listening, *listen*. Don't think about your response; just listen. Look the person in the eyes. Be present. See what it feels like to truly be present with someone. That feeling is *connection*. The people you love to spend time with are probably also doing that for you. Notice it and appreciate it.

3. When you go to a grocery store, restaurant, bank, post office, etc., look at the person who is helping you. Recognize that they are there to help you in some way, and focus on that connection. These are people, not robots; they deserve your connection too. Notice how different it feels to connect with these people, if only for a few moments. If someone appears frazzled or rude, consider that they may be having a bad day.

4. Unplug for a while every day to connect with the people who are physically in your presence. You can also do this to become more connected to yourself. Spend some time meditating, or appreciating all you have to be grateful for. Be sure to appreciate your newfound connections.

5. Devote ten minutes a day of focused attention to each child or other family members that are in your home. Spend this time to reconnect. No judgment, criticism or complaining. You can do an activity that you enjoy together, or just talk.

Change

"I like understanding that things are always evolving, and while there are many things that could be better where I am, it is not really a problem because "where I am" is constantly changing to something better."

— *Abraham Hicks*

Change is the only constant in life. This simple fact is exactly what we need to remind ourselves when we are in the midst of a struggle. We always do manage to handle whatever comes our way. Even in the most difficult of circumstances, we somehow manage to find our way through.

At the extreme, are the losses we experience. When faced with them we feel as though our lives will never be okay again. I distinctly remember feeling that way during the most difficult losses in my life. It is a challenge to get through the day. It is hard to find enjoyment in anything. At these times we know that life will never be the same as it once was. We know this, and we grieve for the loss and for the life that we once had. But somehow we do get through. We manage to smile again and laugh again, and life somehow really does go on.

During the tough times in our life, whether it's a trying time at work or a difficult stage in a loved one's life, inevitably these things do pass. If we could only remember that as bad things are happening, then we would cope more easily. I think back on some difficult times I went through, and I remember thinking at the time, "This is my life now. I guess I just have to accept it." While at the moment that was true, over time it did change. Now, when I don't like how things are going, I always try to remind myself of the fact that change is inevitably coming.

I remember a close friend telling me, when her child was very young, that she had heard that whenever a child is going through a difficult stage, they are growing somehow. I always remembered that when my children were young, and inevitably it *was* true. I think, in some ways, it is always true. Remember, our struggles help us grow. Change and struggle lead to growth. You can remember this by visualizing a butterfly in its cocoon struggling to break free. It is the struggle that gives the butterfly's wings the strength to fly. Without the struggle, the butterfly will die.

The nature of life is change. There is always movement, both good and bad. Children grow out of difficult stages; jobs change; people move on; change occurs.

In reading and listening to Esther/Abraham Hicks' work on the Law of Attraction, I remember being struck by the phrase, "Where I am is constantly changing to something better." This thought will get you through those moments that are difficult. The notion that, "Things are always working out for me," is a comforting thought. And the truth is, they often are.

When I reflect on some of the difficult times in my life, I can truthfully say that some good came from my struggles and sometimes something great came from them. Somehow those times always led me to where I needed to be, or to people that would later become important to my family or me. Sometimes there was a lesson that I needed to learn. And sometimes it simply created a greater appreciation for what I have in my life.

I see this with my clients as well. I have had clients who flunked out of college, and while working with them, it became apparent that not only the school but also what they were studying, was all wrong for them. As we worked together, they were able to figure out a better path, one in which they were not only successful but also incredibly happy.

I have had clients who were miserable in their job, and it took them being that miserable to make a change to something more satisfying. Such changes came about *because of* their struggles, not despite them.

Perhaps this is most apparent with clients who come to me when a relationship ends, or they are laid off from a job. At the time, they are understandably overwhelmed with grief. They are devastated by their loss. But in every single case—that's right *every single case*—something better showed up—something that never would have happened had they not gone through the previous loss.

Remember my client who manifested the wonderful relationship? She could never have seen the outcome when she came in. But once she allowed herself to imagine that something good was coming, it showed up. I try to help my clients to recognize this concept. Not initially, of course, since they need to grieve and find validation. But eventually, they learn to see the gift in the pain.

Ultimately, the goal is to recognize the opportunities for growth, beauty, and extraordinary experiences during our struggles. When you get to a point, in the midst of a difficult time, where you can say, "I know this really stinks right now, but I am excited to see what good will come from it, because I know it's coming," you are in a great place to live joyfully.

I was recently sitting in a doctor's office where I overheard a conversation a man was having with a family member on the phone. They were clearly going through a very hard time. It sounded as though there was a lot of tragedy and illness that the family was dealing with. At the end of the conversation, the man smiled and said, "Well we know things have to change at some point. We've had a lot of bad luck, but things have to turn around sometime. That's the nature of things." I was so impressed by his ability to focus on hope for the future while dealing with his hardships.

Consider how we eagerly await the springtime. Spring is such a beautiful time of year. Everything that was dormant in winter begins to come alive. No matter how hard the winter is, we know that eventually, spring will arrive We are aware of this process with the seasons so as winter wears on we find relief in the knowledge that spring is just around the corner.

Life is much the same way, hard times give way to good times, but we don't know the beauty or the gifts that are on their way to us while we are struggling. When our lives are dreary and dull, we may not have the same expectation of something good coming that we have for the springtime.

If we always knew that something wonderful was headed our way, the way we know spring is coming, we might be able to feel a greater sense of ease. It won't necessarily make us less frustrated with our current circumstances (just like we can still be frustrated when there is a snowfall in March) but knowing that there is an end in sight can help to comfort us through the struggle.

If we choose to live our lives with the knowledge that something beautiful is on its way to us, we can live with the same anticipation that we do for spring.

Think back over your life, and take a little inventory of things that went wrong, and how they ultimately worked out. At some point, things somehow got better. At some point, things changed. As you reflect on these circumstances, see if you can find the gifts. The better you become at this, the closer you will be to helping yourself through any struggle you are going through now and in the future.

If you are having a hard time with this, ask someone close to you to help you. Sometimes we are too close to a situation to see things clearly. If you only have one or two situations that you can think of, focus on those. At the very least, remind yourself that you did get through somehow, and that shows you that you are stronger than you thought you were. Remind yourself that change is constant. Use this knowledge to support and comfort yourself through adversity. Recognize and celebrate the strength you have shown in the past.

Change is your friend. Change means things are getting better and better. And when they aren't, they will be.

Joyful Action Steps: Change

1. Recognize that change is inevitable.

2. Understand that there is always a gift in every struggle.

3. Remember the moments when change was difficult and led to something wonderful; the relationship that ended and led to a better relationship; the job you lost that allowed you to pursue something better; the friendship that developed when you were in the midst of despair. Just like the butterfly, your struggle is part of your journey.

4. Develop a mantra to help you through difficult or changing times. "Whatever happens, I know I can handle it," "Change is my friend" or "Somewhere in here is a gift I'm waiting to discover." Post these (or create your own) prominently in your home or put them on sticky notes wherever you will see them. Let them remind you that things will get better.

5. Give yourself credit for everything you have endured in life up until now. You are so much stronger than you give yourself credit for. Honor the strength within you and your ability to not only survive through change but to thrive through it.

Mindful Breathing

"Feelings come and go like clouds in a windy sky. Conscious breathing is my anchor."

— *Thich Nhat Hanh*

Breathing is the simplest way to calm your body and your mind. But many of us are not sure how, or forget how, to breath properly. Be aware of improper breathing (chest breathing) and replace it with diaphragmatic breathing (belly breathing.) A good way to check your breathing is to lie down and place a book, or even a stuffed animal, on your belly. Breathe in through your nose, and watch your belly rise. Most people "chest breathe,' or breathe shallowly into their chest, which can create more anxiety. Some of us go through our lives never breathing properly.

We are born knowing how to breathe. Watch a baby breathing perfectly with their belly rising and falling. But as we grow, we begin to hold our breath in response to stress and breathe quickly and shallowly. Proper breathing will provide your body with the oxygen you need and help calm you down.

Spend two minutes just following your breath. No need to breathe deeply. Just pay attention to your natural breathing. Notice as you breathe in and as you breathe out. Be aware of your breath. This is the simplest form of meditation. Doing this for two minutes will increase your productivity and happiness and decrease your stress.

Another breathing exercise you can try when under stress is three deep breaths. Breathe in deeply and slowly to a count of four. Hold the breath for a count of four, and exhale slowly to a count of seven. Do this three times, and watch as your stress melts away.

It is hard to be joyful when you are stressed. Breathing is the easiest stress reduction tool you can learn. You can do it anywhere. It requires no special tools, and it costs absolutely nothing. I have taught these simple techniques to many of my clients, and they consistently report success with them. Even my clients with rage issues have used these simple techniques with great success. I recommend getting into a habit of mindful breathing. Find a consistent time to do this. Example times that have worked for my clients are:

- Before getting out of bed
- Whenever you sit down in your car before you put on your seatbelt
- Before you get out of your car at work
- Before you get out of your car at home
- Every time you stop at a red light
- When you take your lunch break
- When you lie down in bed at night

When you choose specific times to practice breathing, it becomes easier to remember and make it part of your day. I like the idea of doing this at all of these times, but it's okay if you only choose one or two to start. You will add more later on because you will see how well it works, and you will be motivated to do this more often.

Here's what you can look forward to when you do two minutes of breathing exercises:

1. When you do your breathing before you get out of bed, you are getting your morning off to a calm start. You will be calmer with your family, roommate, significant other, your children, etc.

2. When you do your breathing when you get in your car, you are allowing yourself to drive calmer and more focused.

3. When you breathe before you get out of your car at work (when you put your car in park), you are inoculating yourself against stress before you enter your workplace. You are setting yourself up for a better day, and you are more prepared to deal with whatever comes your way.

4. When you breathe before you enter your home at the end of the day, (when you turn off your car or before you put your key in the door), you are inserting a pause and creating a calm transition point from work to home. Take that moment to release the stress from the day and be more present with your family. Your family will thank you.

5. When you breathe at every red light, you are developing a visual association to pause and relax. The red light, which means "STOP" becomes your cue to "Stop and breathe." It helps you to create a healthy habit.

6. When you breathe at your lunch break, you are taking a moment to relax and not just eat. You will be calmer, eat more slowly, get less indigestion, and return to work calmer and more productive.

7. When you breathe when you lie down to go to sleep, you are calming your body and your mind. Doing so will allow you to fall asleep more quickly and help you to sleep more soundly.

Two minutes. That's right, just two minutes can have that much of an impact on your life. My clients of all ages return to the breathing exercises because they work, they are easy to do, and they are easy to fit into their day. Even the younger kids I see will do breathing exercises to help them cope with the stress of school and homework.

When you decide that you are going to breathe every time you [Fill in the blank], you create a reminder for yourself. When you sit in your car, that action becomes a reminder to breathe. When you put your car in park, that action becomes a reminder to breathe. You want to create an association, so it becomes second nature.

We are all breathing every day. Focusing our attention on proper breathing takes no extra time. As we become accustomed to breathing properly, we will notice when we are holding our breath, and return to a better breathing rhythm quickly.

Joyful Action Steps: Mindful Breathing

1. Pick one or two times that you are going to devote to mindful breathing. During that time notice your breath for two minutes. Make sure you are breathing all the way into your belly.

   - Before getting out of bed

   - Whenever you sit down in your car, before you put on your seatbelt or when you sit down on the bus or train

   - Before you get out of your car at work

   - Before you get out of your car at home

   - Every time you stop at a red light

   - When you take your lunch break

2. Commit to letting this time be a reminder to you to breathe mindfully for two minutes to calm your body and your mind.

3. Notice how much calmer your day is when you are practicing breathing mindfully.

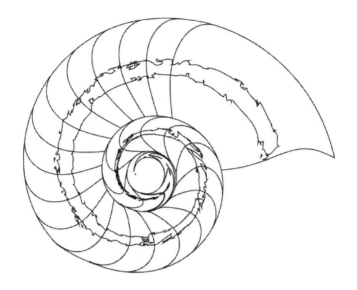

Expand Your Comfort Zone

"Move out of your comfort zone. You can only grow if you are willing to feel awkward and uncomfortable when you try something new."

— Brian Tracy

A joyful life is waiting for you, and it's just outside of your comfort zone!

Why is moving out of your comfort zone important? The most obvious reason is that it is the only way you will grow. Why is growth so critical to joy? I find that boredom can often be an element of sadness or lack of joy. We are meant to continue to learn throughout our lives. Research has shown that learning new things can aid in the prevention of dementia. People are encouraged to keep their minds active and learn new things as they age. Active learning is important for our brains.

We can become creatures of habit doing the same things day after day. There *is* joy in many of our daily activities such as reading to a child, watching a favorite show, or snuggling with a significant other or pet. But we must also continue to grow, or our lives can feel stagnant. I don't think you would have purchased this book if the status quo brought you all the joy you needed.

What is your comfort zone? Imagine a circle on the floor surrounding where you are standing. Inside that circle are all the things you do that you are totally comfortable doing—things that don't cause you anxiety when you think about them. Now outside of that circle is everything else; anything that you would like to do but you haven't for some reason; everything that scares you but excites you as well. If you were to step out of that circle (out of your comfort zone), it would be uncomfortable, awkward, or even scary. But every time you do something that challenges you, you expand your comfort zone.

I encourage people to step outside a little at a time. If there is something that scares you a little, like trying a new food, start with that. Work up to the big things like speaking in front of a group or skydiving.

Doing things that scare you is how you become less fearful. Think about all of the things that were so scary to you at first, like riding a bike, going to school, learning to drive, your first job interview, your first job, your first kiss or first date. There are so many things that we do with ease now, that at one time or another scared or intimidated us. Over time, the more we did them, the more comfortable we became.

"Do one thing every day that scares you."
— Eleanor Roosevelt

A young client of mine suffers from anxiety. She was starting a new job and was very anxious about it. It was not her first job, so we talked about how nervous she was when she started her first job, and how comfortable it became after a while. I reminded her that she would feel the same way with the new job. She was learning to expand her comfort zone—to become more comfortable pushing herself to do things that seem scary at first.

When I was in college, I took a required speech class for my communications degree. I never had any desire to speak in front of groups of people. I had no intention of giving speeches in my career. I was always very anxious before every speech, and I couldn't wait for the class to be over, but as time went on, I started to enjoy the class more and more.

Later, when I became a social worker, my first job required me to deliver employee orientations, supervisory trainings, and staff development programs. I'm not going to lie; I was a nervous wreck every time I did a program. I worried that people would judge me or not like me for some reason. The more I did these programs, the more comfortable I became doing them. I eventually came to love that part of my job, and to this day I still enjoy doing workshops and conferences. I would be lying if I said I didn't get nervous any more. But it's more of an excited nervousness. It's what motivates me to be well prepared. And I feel a sense of satisfaction afterward for doing something that challenges me. The more you push yourself beyond your comfort zone, the more you will feel that way too.

Psychologist Abraham Maslow identified a hierarchy of human needs that he illustrated in a pyramid. The needs, listed from the bottom up were: physiological, safety, love/belonging, esteem, and at the top of the pyramid was self-actualization. Self-actualization refers to our need for personal growth and development throughout our lives. So it makes sense that stepping out of our comfort zone is so important to creating joy.

I find that the accomplishments I am most proud of are those that challenged me and pushed me the most. I see the same with my clients. As they develop new skills and push themselves beyond their comfort zones, they gain a feeling of pride in themselves. This growth leads to a greater sense of satisfaction and a more joyful life.

As you practice stepping out of your comfort zone, it becomes easier to do. When you feel yourself growing, and experience the joy that accompanies it, you will naturally want to stretch yourself more and more. Take the first step, and see if it doesn't help you to feel more joyful.

Joyful Action Steps:
Expanding Your Comfort Zone

Choose from any of these comfort zone expanding actions or come up with your own:

1. Try a new food.

2. Give someone a compliment when you normally wouldn't.

3. Smile and say "Hi" to someone you don't normally talk to.

4. Speak up in a class or group setting when you normally would not speak up.

5. Thank a friend or family member for always supporting you.

6. Let go of your self-judgment for a day, and do something (positive) others would never think you would do.

7. Unplug for a whole day. (No TV, iPad, Laptop, video games, phone).

8. Ask for help.

9. Apologize to someone you have hurt (and admit you were wrong), either in person or by letter.

10. Perform a "random act of kindness."

11. Learn to play an instrument or take voice lessons.

12. Learn to play a new game (Chess, Bridge, Backgammon).

13. Learn a new language.

14. Try a new recipe.

15. Get in touch with someone you haven't seen in a while.

16. Apply for a new job.

17. Start your own business.

18. Write a book.

19. Join a gym or a team.

20. Take up photography or gardening.

21. Take a different route to work.

22. Volunteer at a shelter or a soup kitchen.

23. Become friends with someone who is different than you.

24. Plan an exotic vacation (even if you can't go).

25. Track down a teacher who impacted you, and tell them how important they were to you.

26. Get up early to watch the sunrise.

27. Perform at an amateur night or do karaoke.

28. Read at a poetry reading.

Why Not?

"Others have seen what is and asked why. I have seen what could be and asked why not."

— *Pablo Picasso*

I am often amazed by how often the words, "why not" can alter a life. Many times people get caught up in the "I'll nevers" in their lives, such as: "I'll never meet someone," "I'll never be in a better financial situation," "I'll never be a writer," "I'll never lose the weight." Or how about the "I wish I coulds?" "I wish I could sing!" "I wish I could dance!" "I wish I could travel." I wish I could spend more time with my friends." I hear these phrases or similar ones very frequently in my practice. I often challenge these statements with, "Why not? Why can't you do that?" I usually get a reaction that borders on amazement that is usually followed by a whole slew of reasons why he or she can't do or be a certain thing.

Remember my client who thought she would never meet someone? She is one of many clients who thought the same thing. If you remember, I asked why she wouldn't meet someone, and the response was something along the lines of, "Because things don't work out that way for me." Just because things haven't worked out in the past doesn't mean they can't work out in the future.

As you commit to stretch your comfort zone, you may want to use these words frequently. You've always wanted to sing, but you can barely carry a tune? Take some voice lessons. My husband always wanted to play drums but never learned. A couple of years ago my kids and I bought him a drum set for Christmas. He's been taking weekly lessons ever since. He isn't going on tour anytime soon, but he's having fun challenging himself to do something he's always wanted to do. And it's a great stress reliever.

Have you always wanted to travel to Europe and never did? Why not? Start by doing something simple like getting your passport. It will make you feel like a traveler, and if you want to go, you can! If you don't have the extra money yet for the passport, go to a travel agent and get some brochures. If the cost has been stopping you, open a savings account just for the trip. If you put a little bit of money away every week, it will only be a matter of time before you have enough to go. You can start searching online for a trip that sounds appealing. There are so many discount websites that have great deals on vacations. Just start the process of planning a trip and see if it starts to materialize.

Whenever you hear yourself using limiting language, or shooting down a dream you have, try to follow up with, "why not?" I have seen so many people accomplishing things that they never thought they could, and that includes me! My initial thought when asked to face any new challenge, used to be, "why me?" I would shoot myself down and wonder, "Why should I be considered for the challenge?" Then I started to get into the habit of saying, "Why not me?" instead. Why shouldn't I have as much success or happiness as anyone else? Why wouldn't I be able to handle a particular job? Why not?

This simple question can change your life. It will challenge and push you to do things that you want to do. It will encourage you to move out of the safety of your comfort zone, and most importantly, it will move you into a more joyful challenge zone.

Joyful Action Steps: Why Not?

1. Think of something you've always wanted to do. Consider why you haven't done it, then ask yourself, "Why not?"

2. When you catch yourself thinking that things can't go well for you, remember to ask, "Why not?"

3. When you find yourself feeling envy or jealousy about what someone else has or does, consider asking, "Why *not* me?"

4. When an opportunity presents itself that seems scary but exciting, remember to ask, "Why not?"

5. Don't allow any dream, opportunity or passion to die due to fear or feelings of unworthiness. You are worthy of success, greatness, love, and joy as much as anyone else. WHY NOT YOU?

Prioritizing

"The key is not to prioritize what's on your schedule, but to schedule your priorities."

— *Stephen Covey*

How do we know what's important in someone's life? We take a look at how they are spending their time.

All of the things I talked about in the previous chapters will help you to feel more joyful without question, but you must decide that you are going to make your joy a priority. Taking two minutes to breathe properly will calm you down, but if you don't do it, it won't work. The same goes for everything else we've discussed.

When something is important to us, we should make it a priority. However, we don't always value our time or the energy we exert. I am just as guilty of this as anyone. I love to write, and I have been writing books for decades. I always wanted to publish them, but I didn't make that dream a priority. I let other things take priority in my life. Yes, I was raising my children, working in my practice and doing other important things. But I was also wasting a lot of time. I spent countless hours watching TV and on my computer. These activities certainly helped pass the time, and they were often entertaining, but if you asked me, I would never say that I considered them a priority. And yet, I *made* those things a priority in my life. Had I devoted one hour a day towards my books years ago, I would have at least a dozen published by now.

Take an inventory of what you consider important in your life, and then ask yourself if you are making those things a priority. It's very easy to tell if you are; just look at how much time you devote to them.

If you are a parent, you undoubtedly spend a great deal of time helping your child to feel joyful. You help them to pursue their passions, whether they be sports, music, art or something else. You spend money on lessons and classes. You spend your weekends attending games, or concerts or exhibits. You devote your day driving them to practice, etc. You make their joy a priority. But what about you? What about your passions? What about your joy? Can you commit to making you a priority?

The older we get, the more we realize that our time here is limited. We start to rethink things we have taken for granted. Life is too short to spend time with people that make you miserable and to spend all of your time on commitments that aren't important to you. It's time to take back your life. You can do little things to ensure a joyful life for yourself, and still be there for others. In fact, as you develop your greater sense of joy, you model this positive skill to others around you. As you create a greater sense of joy in your life, the Law of Attraction naturally brings more people who want to experience joy *to* you. You also become much nicer to be around, and perhaps your joy will rub off on the people with whom you spend the most time.

Many years ago, I had a conversation with a friend of mine. We were surprised by how quickly ten years had passed. We discussed how the next ten years could go by just as quickly (and the next, and the next). Our families were our priority, but we didn't want to wake up when we were fifty or sixty to find our dreams for ourselves had passed us by. We had no regrets about the time we devoted to our families. We enjoyed being moms and doing things for our kids and our husbands. But we needed to also think about *our* lives.

Since then, I did make a lot of changes in my life. I developed my practice and started a company with a friend. I started attending workshops and activities that interested me. I developed new interests, and I spent a lot of time being excited about my life. But still, I pushed aside some of my dreams out of fear of judgment, fear of failure, and maybe even just plain laziness. But the bottom line is that I didn't make them a priority.

So the next time you find yourself thinking you don't have time, think again. Yes, time is limited! We only have so much time in each day. However, *you* get to decide how you spend that time. I know that when I made the commitment to pursue my interests, goals, and dreams, my house was a little messier (there are dishes in the sink right now as I write this). But by prioritizing my passions over a perfectly clean house, I've expanded my joy, and I've learned not to take my time for granted. You shouldn't either.

At the beginning of this book, you set an intention to create a more joyful life, don't forget to make *your* joy a priority. Take the time you need to have the life *you* want.

Joyful Action Steps: Prioritizing

At the beginning of this book, I asked you to make a list of things you love to do, people you love to spend time with, etc. It is now time to make all of these things a priority in your life. I want you to consider the action steps in previous chapters. Which actions have brought you the most joy? If you have been implementing these actions in your life, you are probably feeling more joyful. The goal is to keep it up. Throughout your life, there will always be things to derail you. You may not always have time to do all the things you want to do. But every day has the same amount of time—twenty-four hours. And each week contains one hundred and sixty-eight hours. There are things you can do every day—like mindful breathing—and there are things you can commit to weekly—like a scheduled time to connect with people important to you, or a 30-minute weekly music lesson. It is your job to fill those hours in the most joy-filled way possible. Here are some ideas to help you:

1. Make a list of the things you value in your life

    - Family

    - Friends

- Work

- Health

- Spirituality

- Hobbies/Personal Growth

- Vacations

2. Consider things you enjoy doing with the people in your life.

3. Consider your passions and interests.

4. Consider places you'd like to visit.

5. Keep this list in an accessible place.

6. Schedule these things in your calendar; repeating as necessary. If there is a big trip that you'd like to take, but you know you can't do it right away, schedule it for a couple of years from now.

7. Every week on a set day (such as Friday or Sunday) review your week and see if it matches with your values and your priorities. Take note of the ways you prioritized well and be sure to keep them up. Take note of the areas that have been neglected and review your schedule for the coming week. How can you re-prioritize to include those things that are lacking?

8. Remember, the way you spend your time is how you are prioritizing. One less hour spent watching TV every week can give you time to pursue an interest that you "haven't had time for." Your time is a gift, and it is limited, spend it wisely.

Some Final Thoughts

"Focus on the journey, not the destination. Joy is found not in finishing an activity but in doing it."

— *Greg Anderson*

As we travel on life's journey, we will experience many things. We will see miracles, and we will see tragedy. Every single step of our journey serves a purpose. As we learn to appreciate all of the aspects of life, we develop a new relationship with the world around us. We begin to realize that we have more of a say in how we feel than we may have thought. We start to understand that our perception helps to create our reality. I know that I am not the same person I was twenty, or even five years ago. I used to wish that I knew then, what I know now, but I've come to realize that it's not meant to be that way.

Every time someone I love is struggling or unhappy, I wish I could take the pain away. That hasn't changed. But I remind myself that the struggle is part of the journey. We are changed by our experiences. How we change is up to us.

By choosing to recognize the gifts or lessons in our struggles, to see the beauty in the every day and to create meaningful connections, we allow ourselves not just to live, but also to thrive. As we practice the skills we learn, we create a more positive and hopeful outlook, and we can begin to experience joy on a deeper level. We experience joy that transcends the moment.

When you live your life joyfully, you have so much more to give. Through your connection, laughter, compassion and love you are sending the energy of joy out into the world. I think the world could use as much joy as it can get. I would love to hear about your journey to joy. Please feel free to contact me to share how *Journey to Joy* helped you.

Recommended Reading

The Law of Attraction

- *The Secret*, by Rhonda Byrne
- *The Power*, by Rhonda Byrne
- *The Magic*, by Rhonda Byrne
- *Co-creating at its Best: A Conversation Between Master Teachers*, by Dr. Wayne Dyer and Esther Hicks
- *Ask, and it is Given*, by Esther Hicks

Intention

- *The Hidden Messages in Water*, by Dr. Masaru Emoto
- *Love Thyself*, by Dr. Masaru Emoto
- *The Intention Experiment*, by Lynne McTaggert

Parenting

- *Smart Love: The Compassionate Alternative to Discipline That Will Make You a Better Parent and Your Child a Better Person*, by Martha Heineman Pieper and William J. Pieper

Success in Life

- *The Success Principles*, by Jack Canfield
- *The Magic of Conflict*, by Tom Crum

Self-Compassion

- *The Forgotten Friend*, by Janice Fuchs

Compassion Fatigue

- *Compassion Fatigue*, by Charles Figley
- *Secondary Traumatic Stress*, by Beth Stamm
- *Trauma and the Therapist*, by Laurie Pearlman & Karen Saakvitne

Breaking Out of Your Comfort Zone

- *Feel the Fear and Do it Anyway*, by Susan Jeffers

About the Author

Susan Goryeb Simms, LCSW, has been a clinical psychotherapist for more than 25 years. She earned her MS degree in Social Work in 1990 from Columbia University. Susan has conducted numerous workshops and presented at conferences on such topics as stress management, cultural diversity, parenting and work/life balance. As founder of **Positive Therapy 4 U**, Susan provides inspiration and validation for people around the world. She is also co-founder of **Indigo Light Center for Joyful Living** where she conducts groups and workshops for children, teens, and adults on mindfulness, meditation, managing stress and other related topics.

Susan has the privilege of helping her clients heal from a variety of problems. She works with individuals, families, couples and groups. Her extensive knowledge of stress management methods, including mind/body techniques such as guided meditation, mindfulness, and EFT, are incorporated in her eclectic approach.

Susan combines the tools presented in this book with strength-based, supportive counseling to help her clients transform limiting beliefs and patterns, enabling them to thrive, leading happier, more fulfilling lives. She has seen incredible transformations occur when her clients begin to apply what they've learned.

Susan has a passion for inspiring and empowering people to be their most joyful and compassionate version of themselves. It is her wish in writing *Journey to Joy: Insights and Actions for a Happier Life*, to reach more people and to help them create a life of joy.

Susan lives with her husband, Kevin, and her children, Jess and Nick in their home in Long Island, NY. They also have a puppy, Leia, who, despite her craziness (or because of it), brings them a great deal of joy.

You can find Susan at her website, **PositiveTherapy4U.com** and on her Facebook pages: **Positive Therapy 4 U** and **Indigo Light Center for Joyful Living**.

99105402R00095

Made in the USA
Columbia, SC
09 July 2018